From Exposed To Secure

FROM

E**X**POSED

TO

SECURE

**The Cost Of Cybersecurity And
Compliance Inaction And The Best Way
To Keep Your Company Safe**

Featuring Cybersecurity & Compliance Experts
From Around The World

NEW YORK

LONDON • NASHVILLE • MELBOURNE • VANCOUVER

From Exposed To Secure

The Cost Of Cybersecurity And Compliance Inaction And The Best Way To Keep Your Company Safe

Published in New York, New York, by Morgan James Publishing. Morgan James is a trademark of Morgan James, LLC. www.MorganJamesPublishing.com

Proudly distributed by Publishers Group West®

ISBN 9781636983851 paperback
ISBN 9781636983868 ebook
Library of Congress Control Number:
9781636983868

Cover Design by:
Caitlin Lawless, Senior Graphic Designer
Big Red Media

Interior Design by:
Christopher Kirk
www.GFSstudio.com

Morgan James is a proud partner of Habitat for Humanity Peninsula and Greater Williamsburg. Partners in building since 2006.

Get involved today! Visit: www.morgan-james-publishing.com/giving-back

TABLE OF CONTENTS

Chapter 1

THE CYBERSECURITY TRAP: WHY CYBERSECURITY AND CYBER COMPLIANCE ARE NOT THE SAME

Wayne Hunter

You can have cybersecurity without compliance. But you can't have regulatory compliance without cybersecurity. A lot of people confuse this, which can lead to expensive lessons. Make no mistake; you cannot afford to skip educating yourself on this topic because not understanding the difference can and will cost you. Even the financial industry, one of the most regulated industries, has been fined $243 billion since 2008.

Cybercrime is at an all-time high, leading organizations to tighten compliance requirements. According to a report on crime syndicates, over 60% of financial institutions around the world have been hit with sophisticated cyberattacks intended to take over brokerage accounts so they can sneak into banks to steal money. The overriding conclusion from financial sector CISOs and security leaders is that financial institutions are increasingly imperiled by ransomware using new target marketing strategies. Indeed, 74% experienced at least one ransomware attack over the last year, with 63% coughing up the demanded ransom.[1]

But it would be foolish to assume that these kinds of hits are only happening in financial institutions or companies with more money.

Cybersecurity is an area that affects businesses of *all* sizes, including small businesses, which are the target of almost half of all cyberattacks.[2] However, most businesses don't understand that cybersecurity is only one part of the equation and that compliance is equally important.

As an MSP helping businesses of all sizes with their compliance, including those in the highly regulated financial and Department of Defense (DoD) industries, I've seen what happens when business owners fall into the cybersecurity trap by either ignoring compliance or believing compliance doesn't apply to their business.

There are many compliance rules out there. Not only are more compliance policies being put in place, but these policies are also being enforced. Recently, the FTC Safeguards Rule began requiring covered companies to develop, implement, and maintain an information security program with administrative, technical, and physical safeguards designed to protect customer information. Ignoring this rule can result in significant penalties of up to $100,000 per violation and damage your business's reputation. A lot of people thought this rule only applied to financial institutions, such as banks, or that it was hype. However, it applies to nonbanking financial institutions, including brokerage houses, mortgage companies, motor vehicle dealers, and payday lenders. The rule lists them, but if you don't read it, how would you know? Before we get into how you can avoid falling into this trap, let's look at the difference between cybersecurity and compliance.

What Is Cybersecurity?

Cybersecurity is the protection of computer systems, networks, and data from unauthorized access, attacks, and damage. In other words, "What am I implementing to secure my environment? And am I maintaining that?"

What Is Compliance?

Compliance is an established framework of regulations, standards, and policies that must be followed to ensure your data remains safe. Compliance determines whether the cybersecurity measures you have in place comply with the rules or laws based on regulations or requirements from state and federal laws and your industry. In other words, "Am I doing the things required for me to be compliant with those frameworks and policies?"

Requirements Beyond Cybersecurity Protection Make Up Compliance

A big mistake people make is thinking that because they've put cybersecurity protections in place, they are compliant. Of course, when looking at whether you are compliant, the first thing that will be checked is whether you've got the security pieces put in place. But that's only a small piece of compliance. Other questions include:

- Do you have cybersecurity policies?
- Do you have a bring-your-own-device policy?
- Do you have an incident response plan?
- Do you have a business continuity plan?
- Are you doing cyber training for your users? (The #1 way businesses get hacked is through their employees clicking on something they shouldn't, which is why education is a requirement for compliance.)
- Are your vendors meeting your requirements from a security posture standpoint, and are you tracking it?

That's compliance. So, you've got to have cybersecurity to do compliance. But you can't do compliance without doing these other things as well.

What's the Difference Between Cybersecurity and Compliance?

While a business can *say* they are taking the necessary cybersecurity protection measures, compliance is *proof* that they are doing so.

When looking at services an MSP/MSSP will offer, basic cybersecurity services include firewalls, antivirus protection, patching updates, user management, and advanced security. You might also have advanced cybersecurity services that include identity access management (IAM), domain name system (DNS) filters, a secure virtual private network (VPN), SOC-as-a-Service (SOCaaS), and incident response (IR).

Compliance-as-a-Service (CaaS) will include:

- Aligning compliance requirements with cybersecurity systems and controls
- Identifying gaps in compliance
- Documentation, including validated evidence of compliance
- Audits and certification preparation for compliance frameworks, such as CMMC (Cybersecurity Maturity Model Certification) and NIST 800-171 (National Institute of Standards and Technology), FTC Safeguards, and IRS 4557

Why Compliance Must Be a Priority

Every Business Has Base Compliance Requirements

Hacking is not discriminatory. Payouts for ransomware are happening across all industries. Because of these payouts, cybersecurity insurance providers are tightening requirements. Base requirements must be met across every business, with even more requirements depending on the industry you're in. For example, in banking, there are FDIC requirements; with the DoD, CMMC compliance must be met. These industries extend compliance further because of certain data requirements. If you can't prove you are following the requirements, many insurance companies won't even consider writing you a policy. If you can get a cybersecurity policy and need to file a claim, underwriters are going to scrutinize your compliance. If you don't have policies and procedures in place, it's going to cost you even more.

This is why you must constantly look to find out what is happening that may affect your business. There are four different areas you'll want to monitor: federal, state, industry, and cybersecurity.

At the state level, cybersecurity acts are in place, such as the SHIELD Act in New York and the California Consumer Privacy Act in California. Other states are also starting to adopt their own state cyber acts. Businesses must comply with these state regulations. If no state regulation is in place, you must comply with federal regulations.

This is a lot to monitor, which can be overwhelming, especially while you're trying to run your business. But if you don't keep up with these compliance requirements, it's going to be difficult to run your business. The good news is that there are qualified MSP/MSSP businesses that specialize in compliance-as-a-service and can help you with compliance changes and requirements.

Compliance Will Only Get More Expensive If You Wait

Compliance isn't going away. While everybody has budgets, getting compliant now is much cheaper than doing it later. If you think you can avoid compliance by just paying a fine, think again. With cybersecurity, you may get away with paying a fine that isn't that much. But noncompliance can result in much higher costs to your business, including loss of reputation and business due to that noncompliance.

Another thing to consider is your clients. It doesn't matter if you're a small company that doesn't have a lot of money. Most small to medium businesses (SMBs) have access to anywhere from a single client contact to around 200 client contacts. A hacker will look for ways to access these contacts to gain access to bigger fish. For example, they might access information through your QuickBooks.

This is causing businesses, vendors, and agencies you interact with to monitor their business partners' compliance with cybersecurity to protect their interests and reputation. More and more businesses are asking their vendors of all sizes, "Do you have a cyber policy? Do you have an incident response plan? What happens when we are sharing information?" It is becoming more common to see clauses in contracts that require compliance, and, as a safety measure, a third-party cybersecurity risk assessment may even be required to prove you are complying.[3] If you're not in compliance, they won't do business with you.

Unfortunately, a lot of small companies have gone out of business because they thought compliance wouldn't impact them.

There is a good chance you are already not in compliance in a way that could have consequences. The IRS is sending letters to CPAs and bookkeeping clients asking for confirmation that these business owners are compliant with certain requirements, such as whether they are securing their clients' taxpayer data. When our CPA and bookkeeping clients received this letter, we compared requirements and confirmed that the IRS rules are being pulled from NIST requirements. This indicates other agencies will follow, meaning it's going to grow and get more complex. Plus, this compliance issue doesn't just apply to CPAs and bookkeepers. It applies to anybody or any company that has any tax information about an employee.

Sooner or later, this will impact you. It's best to get everything in place now because the compliance mountain is only going to get bigger.

Changes in Compliance Are Happening All the Time

Compliance is not something you look at just once a year. In the compliance environment, changes happen quickly. In the banking industry, changes happen so fast that they go out of compliance and don't even realize it. Utilizing compliance-as-a-service can reduce compliance fines because an MSP/MSSP can monitor changes so you know exactly when you go out of compliance and can stay on top of addressing changes to bring you back into compliance.

It's the Law, Not Optional

Compliance is the law regarding what you must have in place pertaining to your cyber-security measures, policies, and plans. You must prove you're following the policies for compliance in your business environment and prove you are maintaining them.

Regulatory agencies around the world are putting pressure on businesses to establish a more proactive approach to compliance regarding data privacy and cybersecurity best practices.

By neglecting these legal mandates, you increase your risk of an audit and hefty violation penalties, potential litigation, severe reputation damage—which could lead to a loss of trust and your customers—and, ultimately, even jail time.

Good News: Compliance Isn't Something You or Your IT Department Do Alone

Don't fall into the cybersecurity trap of thinking you are good simply because you have cybersecurity protections in place. Educate yourself on compliance and make sure you are following the established compliance framework for your business environment.

Do your homework, but don't expect to understand everything you need to know about compliance. It's a complicated topic and a full-time endeavor to keep up with the constant changes. The good news is you don't have to do this alone. If you're not sure and your IT team doesn't know, don't be afraid to get help. The best first step is to contact a qualified MSP/MSSP that understands compliance and the compliance requirements for your business environment and get an assessment. The MSP/MSSP will help you understand where you are now, where you need to be, and how to get there. For example, my company, AvTek Solutions, Inc., offers assessments that also include customized education on compliance for your specific business environment and recommendations on what to do to get compliant.

If you have cybersecurity insurance or are applying for a cybersecurity insurance policy, the insurance company will ask you specific questions about what you have in place. Their questions can be used as a free cybersecurity policy review that won't cost you a dime. They will tell you what your policy is, what your requirements are, and what you would need to pay out. At a minimum, you'll know where you stand. At maximum, you end up with a cybersecurity policy that will give you further protection and will help satisfy a mandate many vendors are beginning to require.

Every business owner needs to be aware of compliance. If you have even one 1099 employee, you've got Personal Identifiable Information (PII), which means there is compliance you must follow. If you are not putting policies in place and don't have cybersecurity insurance, you could find yourself being denied work. You must do compliance.

Get a qualified company involved that is doing compliance full-time to help guide you and prepare you. When you know what you need to do, you're better prepared, and when you're better prepared, it will cost you less money.

About Wayne

Wayne Hunter is the co-founder and CEO of AvTek Solutions, Inc., an Amazon #1 bestselling author, a speaker, and a leader in the IT industry. Providing cutting-edge information technology solutions to customers, he brings over thirty years of experience and expertise to the table. Focused on storage and data systems, IT management and systems integration, and mitigating risk, Wayne has a passion for solving IT problems, which has established a reputation of trust in him among colleagues and customers. His mission is to provide the best possible solution to every customer, with a vision of tying his customers' success directly to AvTek's success.

Prior to starting AvTek Solutions, Wayne served six years in the Navy, where he spent two years going through the Navy's Electronics Training Program (one of the best training programs in the world) and four years on the USS *Dallas* (SSN 700) submarine. After the Navy, Wayne worked for a supercomputer company in Dallas, Texas, where he noticed many businesses didn't have the technology in place to address their large-scale automated backup operation requirements. In response, he launched Lexicon Information Concepts, LLC, which, after seven years of success, he sold to one of his vendors, Legato Systems, Inc. Wayne continued as Legato's Vice President of Customer Solutions and then as Vice President of Enterprise Solutions when Legato was purchased by EMC. Soon after the acquisition, he realized that entrepreneurship was in his blood, leading him to co-found AvTek Solutions in 2004.

With over ten years of experience specializing in banks, Wayne has led AvTek to become one of the premier IT experts in the financial services industry. As a veteran who is always willing to adapt to the ever-changing technology landscape, Wayne quickly put the wheels in motion for AvTek to become a Cybersecurity Maturity Model Certification Registered Provider Organization to help Department of Defense contractors and subcontractors become CMMC compliant when the DoD announced CMMC back in 2020.

Wayne stays ahead of the curve and ensures he brings the right type of technology to his clients to keep them up to date by serving on boards such as the Cytracom Partner Advisory Council, which is a leading voice focused on driving the best future for modern communications, the Channel Company XChange Advisory Board and the technical advisory board of the American Standard Code for Information Interchange

(ASCII) Group. He has also been tapped into for his cybersecurity and compliance expertise and has co-authored two previous books: *Exploited!* and *The Compliance Formula: Successful Strategies of CMMC Compliant Companies.*

In the community, Wayne is a longtime supporter of the Special Olympics and St. Jude Children's Research Hospital. He also supports his clients' community services in any way he can. For instance, along with Austin Bank employees, Wayne helped build beds for children at homeless shelters. Wayne and Susan, his wife of thirty-six years, live on a thirty-four-acre Texas farm, where they enjoy time on the lake or in the woods. You can also catch them at a Rangers game.

For more information, contact Wayne at AvTek Solutions, Inc.:

Email: wayne.hunter@avteksolutions.com
Phone: (214) 778-2983
Web: www.avteksolutions.com

Chapter 2

WHY SMALL BUSINESSES ARE A CYBERCRIMINAL'S #1 TARGET
Konrad Martin

H indsight is a funny thing. It'd be life-changing to have access to it before you make any critical life choices. But, of course, it doesn't work like that.

If you are a small business owner, you may think your company is too small to be noticed by cybercriminals. Unfortunately, nothing could be further from the truth. Criminals have homed in on smaller companies as their prime targets. In fact, small businesses are three times more likely to be targeted by cybercriminals than larger companies.[4] To help you vastly reduce your chances of becoming another victim of malicious activities online, here are eleven reasons small to medium-sized business (SMB) operators are an easy target for cybercrime:

1. **Lack of awareness.** Nearly 60% of SMB owners believe their business is unlikely to be targeted by cybercriminals.[5] While alarming, it's not surprising. When you read the news, nobody's mentioning that twenty-member CPA firm that got hacked or that fifteen-member financial planning practice that sent money to the wrong person. It's not that it doesn't happen. It's that the news believes these stories are too small to cover. And because we haven't read about the 700,000+ SMBs hacked during the year, we think small businesses are not the target.
2. **Lack of education.** While education is available through managed services providers (MSPs) and managed security services providers (MSSPs), the edu-

cation about what SMBs need in order to secure their business and which compliance policies apply to them is not mainstream enough to be on most SMBs' radar. When COVID required people to work from home, cyber-criminals targeted small businesses in a big way because SMBs didn't know they needed to have policies in place for working from home. Therefore, unlike large organizations, which require steps that employees need to take just to log in, SMBs didn't know to tell employees not to go home without a company-issued laptop or that they needed to make sure their employees didn't just use any device to log into the company network.

3. **Lack of proper security.** The majority of SMBs are not prepared for a cyber-attack and have weaker defenses than enterprise companies. This may be due to business owners' lack of awareness about the need for additional security measures beyond antivirus protection, such as a complete security stack, or the risk to their security stack. And cybercriminals know it. This is unfortu-nate because while securing data can be simple, remediation in the event of an attack is not. Companies that suffer from a cyberattack experience signif-icant downtime, which impacts productivity, lost data, and lost revenue, not to mention damage to their reputation.

4. **No dedicated security and compliance policy administrator.** Fewer than 10% of SMBs have a dedicated IT staff member,[6] whereas larger companies often hire a dedicated administrator whose sole responsibility is cybersecu-rity and compliance policies. No business, not even a small business, oper-ates in a silo. There are constant changes to compliance, new technologies being introduced, or new situations that require attention. Take the work-from-home example: SMBs didn't have a person to create policies for how employees should work from home. Or look at the new technology that is introduced all the time—anything that has a microchip and can connect to the Internet is fair game for a cybercriminal. For instance, without proper security measures in place, a Ring doorbell can easily be hacked.

    Fortunately, an MSP or MSSP can serve as a dedicated person to help small businesses with cybersecurity and compliance policies.

5. **Lack of resources.** Even if SMBs know they should have more robust cyber-security and compliance protocols in place, they often lack a pocketbook large enough to protect themselves all the time. For example, a ten-person

financial company may have to pay $500 for the security stack. Plus, they need the right tools in place for compliance to qualify for cybersecurity insurance. (Some vendors now require cyber insurance to do business with them.) Managing their security stack, implementing policies, providing training to employees, conducting simulated phishing emails to ensure safety, and following compliance measures often increase the cost.

That means it can get expensive. But it's *outrageously* expensive without it if an SMB gets attacked, and this can even force SMBs to go out of business. Around 64% of small businesses that get hacked don't recover. When a business gets hacked, it loses access to its entire database, and the cybercriminal demands a ransom to regain access, which could be $5,000, $10,000, or even more. They want you to pay in cryptocurrency so it's not trackable, which means you'll need to hire an MSP/MSSP to negotiate with the cybercriminal. My MSP has done this for businesses, and it's not cheap.

Imagine the MSP gets the cybercriminal to be nice. You pay the ransom, they provide the key to get the information back, and the MSP gets everything running again. What's the first thing you do? You go back to the MSP and tell them you want to implement the security stack and everything you said you couldn't afford before. Only now, you've doubled your costs because of what you just paid to the cybercriminal. And that's if everything goes well. A lot of times, an MSP can't get the information back, and if it's backed up, it can take days to get that information off your backups because while backups are designed to completely restore you, they can't accomplish that in one day. You're talking about restoring terabytes of data, which takes time to transfer.

6. **SMBs' failure to budget for protection.** Forty-seven percent of businesses with fewer than fifty employees have no cybersecurity budget.[7] But budgeting for cybersecurity is less expensive than paying to deal with an attack. Think of it this way: no one plans to get sick or hurt, but most people need medical care at some point, so they have health insurance to protect themselves from unexpected, high medical costs.

Similarly, a security stack makes your business much more secure. While it can't guarantee 100% protection from hackers, it can significantly reduce your chances of being breached. Plus, if you are the victim of a cyberattack, the damages and costs are going to be far less than they would be without coverage.

7. **Increased reliance on technology.** Nearly a decade ago, less than half of SMBs claimed to be dependent on their technology. But as of 2023, 93% are now dependent on technology and its applications.[8] Vulnerability to cyberattacks will only increase as more small businesses move their operations to the cloud and adopt advanced technology.

8. **Personal vulnerabilities.** As a small business owner, you don't have just one job to do—you are doing a hundred things at once. You're marketing your business, paying the bills, and finishing that proposal. Cybercriminals know this and use it against you—targeting businesses during high-volume hours such as tax season.

   Embarrassment is also a powerful tool. Cybercriminals bank on people being too embarrassed to report an incident quickly. We do a lot of work with CPAs, and during tax season, a partner at a CPA firm contacted me and said, "I think I have a problem." She'd clicked on a message with a pop-up attachment that said it was a tracking attachment for UPS. Despite not having ordered anything for at least a month, she clicked on the attachment. When I asked her why she had clicked on it, she confessed that curiosity had gotten the best of her. Nothing happened immediately, so she disregarded it. But the next day, she couldn't access her database. She told me she knew she did the wrong thing the minute she clicked on the file but waited to say anything because she was embarrassed. What should have happened, no matter the time of day or night, is that she should have called us. But she didn't. Cybercriminals count on that behavior.

9. **SMBs hold valuable personal information.** Personal information must be treated with the same caution and respect regardless of whether it's your own information or a client's. Personal information, such as credit card details and Social Security numbers, are targets for cybercriminals. Financial professionals, CPAs, doctors, and dentists hold a lot of personal information on clients. Think about it. The last time you went to the dentist, how did you pay? You put it on a credit card. So now the cybercriminal can access your credit card, your first name, your last name, and probably your Social Security number. That valuable information is like gold to cybercriminals.

Even if you're an extremely small business with zero employees, if you invoice a larger client or send documents or communications through email, you are an attractive target because you might hold entryways into larger companies a hacker can exploit.

10. **SMBs are part of a supply chain.** Just as SMBs can crack the door for hackers to enter larger, more valuable companies, SMBs often don't realize they too can fall victim to cybercrime because they are part of a supply chain. Vendors they do business with hold their personal information, which makes the SMB a target if a company they do business with gets hacked. Recently, a hospital was hacked while operations were being performed. They were forced to halt operations until they paid the ransom money. This didn't just shut down the hospital; it allowed the hacker to look inside their supply chain.

11. **Viruses are much more sophisticated.** Gone are the days when you immediately knew you had gotten a virus. Cybercriminals gather intelligence for a considerable amount of time before attempting to extort money. They can even access bank accounts and determine the exact amount of money available so they know how much money they can get from you.

Years ago, when I was working as a CPA, my boss got the "ILOVEYOU" virus. When you clicked on the attachment, it grabbed all your contacts' email addresses and sent a mass email saying, "I love you." You knew you were infected immediately because, within twenty minutes, multiple contacts were calling about it. Today, hackers don't tip their victims off right away. In many cases, SMBs compromised with malware don't discover it for more than two years.[9] While hackers usually don't want to wait too long to trigger a ransomware payload, in case they lose access to the network, they're still perfectly happy staying inside the network for up to six months because there's plenty of money to be gained along the way to the final attack.[10] During this time, bits of information are collected. Now the hacker knows who your clients are, can see deposits, and, over time, can figure out how much money you have in your account. If you only have $15,000 in your account, the hacker is going to ask for that exact amount.

Colonial Pipeline was compromised by a single password on an old, unprotected account. The pipeline virus shut down the gas to the southeastern part of the US and caused spiking gasoline prices, panic buying, and empty gas stations up and down the East Coast. After a six-day shutdown, a $4.4 million ransom was paid to the hackers. Once a virus infiltrates your system like that, it's a lot more difficult to clear out of the system.

Small businesses are at grave risk of cybercrime because they are an easy target. Without the right set of protection tools, more than 60% of SMBs will not recover from a cyberattack. As a small business owner, you must take this seriously and implement cybersecurity and compliance measures because if you don't and you get hit, it's going to devastate your business.

If you don't have cybersecurity and compliance measures in place or aren't sure if you have the right protection and policies, google MSSPs near you, pick up the phone and call them. Talk to someone who understands not only cybersecurity and compliance but also the industry you are in. Most MSPs/MSSPs, like mine, will offer an assessment so you can see where your business stands. Interview a few different MSSPs. Read the Google reviews about the companies you're considering. Call them to see if a real person picks up the phone. You are entrusting them with your business, so in addition to the cybersecurity services they can provide, you want a good rapport and to know that you can easily get in touch with them 24/7 should you encounter a problem.

About Konrad

Konrad Martin is the CEO of Tech Advisors, a firm he founded in 2005 with his twin brother, Kevin. Tech Advisors is a complete technology solutions provider, 100% committed to seeing that business owners have the most reliable, professional IT service. Under Konrad's leadership, the firm has achieved steady growth and expansion of services offered—including cybersecurity, compliance, cloud computing, and more—to growing businesses across a wide range of industries.

Tech Advisors was named one of the world's premier managed services providers (MSPs) in 2022 and 2021 in the prestigious Channel Futures MSP 501 rankings, as well as a Top 250 MSP in 2022 and a Top 250 MSSP (managed security services providers) in 2021. Originally focused on the Greater Boston area, the company has grown to offer services throughout the East Coast and maintains offices in Boston, Massachusetts; Providence, Rhode Island; Marlborough, Massachusetts; and Palm Beach, Florida.

A nationally recognized authority in the field of cybersecurity, Konrad was recently featured in the documentary *Cyber Crime 2: The Dark Web Uncovered*. He and nine other national cybersecurity experts were selected for the film, in which they explore the psychology and techniques of cybercrime and offer tips on how to avoid becoming a victim.

Konrad is also the co-author of *Cyber Storm*, an Amazon #1 bestseller, and the author of *Hacked! How To Protect Your Business from the Fines, Lawsuits, Customer Loss, and PR Nightmare Resulting from Data Breach and Cybercrime*, which offers strategies for staying one step ahead of cybercriminals, and *The IT Factor*, a comprehensive guide for the small business owner who seeks to find a professional, competent IT provider. Konrad has authored additional cybersecurity articles for a number of regional and national magazines and was featured in *MSP Success Magazine*'s spring 2021 special edition with his article "The CPA Turned IT Consultant Every CPA Firm Wants to Know."

Konrad uses his publications and other platforms to educate audiences about the field of cybersecurity and the reality that cybercrime is a sophisticated and organized industry. He believes strongly that education and empathy are critical and that teams that are unified and knowledgeable are the best way to fight against the growing danger.

Before founding Tech Advisors, Konrad worked as a CPA; this background gives him an understanding and appreciation of the financial side of technology, and he enjoys helping Tech Advisors' clients connect the value of a well-managed IT infrastructure with business efficiency and profitability. His background also led him to become a trusted advisor to the Massachusetts Society of CPAs; he wrote the Written Information Security Plan for their organization and its hundreds of members.

The Bangor, Maine, native is a graduate of the University of Maine, where he competed and became a nationally ranked swimmer. He enjoys several outdoor activities, including hiking, golfing, and triathlons. Konrad splits his time between Medway, Massachusetts, and Lantana, Florida, with his wife, Jeannie. They are parents to Rebecca, Adam, and Fritz.

For more information, contact Konrad at Tech Advisors:

Email: konradm@tech-adv.com
Phone: (508) 356-5565
Web: www.tech-adv.com
LinkedIn: www.linkedin.com/in/konrad-martin-1791101/

Chapter 3

WHAT ARE THE BIGGEST CYBERTHREATS THAT COULD TAKE YOUR BUSINESS DOWN?

Pervez Delawalla

In today's Internet-connected world, where technology plays a vital role in our everyday lives, cybersecurity threats have become increasingly sophisticated and prevalent. Whether an individual user or a large corporation, everyone is at risk of a cyberattack. Cybercriminals are becoming more sophisticated, using advanced techniques and psychology to breach networks. These criminals steal sensitive data, causing significant financial damage, and can even destroy reputations. This chapter will explore the top cybersecurity threats that organizations face, discussing their potential impact and offering valuable insights into preventive measures and widely accepted best practices.

Threats: The Overview

The number and type of cyberthreats are constantly changing, growing, and evolving. The complete list is pages long, but I want to give you an overview of some of the most common threats and the basic steps to defend against them. These attacks include phishing, ransomware, Internet of Things (IoT), zero-day, supply chain, and insider threats.

Phishing attacks remain one of the most prevalent cybersecurity threats. Cybercriminals employ deceptive tactics, such as fraudulent emails, messages, or websites, to trick unsuspecting individuals into divulging sensitive information. These attacks target personal data, financial information, and login credentials. To mitigate this threat, it is crucial to exercise caution while interacting with suspicious emails, double-checking the legitimacy of requests, and adopting email filtering systems.

Ransomware attacks have experienced a dramatic rise in recent years, causing significant disruptions across industries. Malicious actors deploy ransomware to encrypt critical data and demand ransom for its release. Victims often face the dilemma of either paying the ransom or suffering severe data loss. To counter this threat, organizations should regularly back up their data, deploy advanced endpoint protection, and implement strong security policies.

The growth of Internet of Things devices has introduced new security challenges. Many IoT devices lack proper security measures, making them attractive targets for cybercriminals. Hacking IoT devices can provide unauthorized access into networks, enabling attackers to gather sensitive data or disrupt operations. To safeguard against IoT vulnerabilities, users must change default device credentials and update firmware regularly.

Zero-day exploits target software vulnerabilities that are unknown to the vendor, leaving organizations vulnerable to attacks. Cybercriminals exploit these vulnerabilities before security patches or updates are released, making them challenging to detect and prevent. Mitigating zero-day exploits involves staying up-to-date with the latest security patches and leveraging intrusion detection systems. You should also keep up with the latest security bulletins.

Supply chain attacks involve compromising a trusted vendor or supplier to gain unauthorized access to target systems. Cybercriminals exploit vulnerabilities in software updates, hardware components, or third-party services to infiltrate the supply chain and install malicious code or backdoors. To protect against supply chain attacks, organizations should conduct thorough checks when selecting vendors, regularly assess and monitor third-party security practices, and implement stringent security controls, including code signing and secure update mechanisms. So, even if you are doing everything correctly at your location, you could still be impacted by a vendor that isn't as diligent.

While external cyberthreats often grab headlines, insider threats pose a significant risk to organizations. Insider threats involve malicious or negligent actions by employees who have authorized access to sensitive systems or information. These individuals may intentionally steal or leak data or unintentionally cause breaches through carelessness. To mitigate insider threats, organizations should implement strong access controls, conduct background checks on employees, monitor user activities, and establish clear security policies.

The Big Bad Wolf Turns CEO

Cybercriminals have evolved into sophisticated entities that operate much like legitimate businesses, leveraging technology and exploiting vulnerabilities to profit from their activities. These modern-day criminals have changed the landscape of crime, conducting their operations with organizational structures, business models, and profit-driven approaches.

First and foremost, cybercriminals exhibit a high level of specialization. Just as legitimate businesses have various departments, cybercriminal organizations are composed of specialists in different areas. There are hackers who develop and deploy malware, programmers who create exploit kits, money mules who facilitate financial transactions, and even customer service representatives who provide technical support to their criminal clientele.

Cybercriminals have established complex supply chains. They buy and sell stolen data, trading in digital marketplaces on the dark web. These underground marketplaces offer a range of products and services, including stolen credentials, credit card information, hacking tools, and even hacking-for-hire services. The cybercriminal network is based on collaboration and partnerships with individuals and groups specializing in different aspects of cybercrime.

To ensure longevity and profitability, cybercriminals invest in research and development. They constantly adapt their tactics and techniques to evade detection by law enforcement and security measures. They innovate new methods of phishing, ransomware attacks, and social engineering to exploit human vulnerabilities. Just like legitimate businesses, cybercriminals try to maintain a competitive edge.

In addition, cybercriminals prioritize cost-effectiveness and return on investment. They conduct risk assessments and calculate potential profits before launching attacks. They may outsource certain tasks to lower-cost regions or employ automation tools to maximize efficiency. These criminal enterprises focus on maximizing revenue and avoiding capture.

Lastly, cybercriminals are beginning to exhibit a customer-oriented approach. They provide user-friendly platforms and services, offering technical support to build trust among their customers. They have chat forums and online communities where aspiring criminals can seek guidance and advice, fostering a sense of community within their network.

Where to Focus

All the threats outlined above are important to guard against. You should do your best to implement strategies that address each of them. Right now, I want to focus on two frauds that are most used by cybercriminals. More specifically, one attack and how they achieve it. I'm talking about ransomware and phishing. Over the last several years, ransomware has become the attack of choice for these organized cybercriminal groups. It often pays the best dividends, and that's increasing as more insurance companies write policies offering ransomware protection.

I've outlined the basics of ransomware earlier in the chapter, but let's get into the details. Ransomware is a type of malware. Malware is a broad definition of malicious software installed on a system without the user's knowledge. Once the malware is installed, it will make its way across your network and encrypt your files. If your backups are accessible from the same network, then they will also encrypt backup files. If they succeed at encrypting your systems and your backups, then choices are limited for restoring your systems. Once your systems are under hacker control, the hackers will demand a ransom to release your files. They will likely request the ransom be paid by cryptocurrency or some other untraceable means. The hackers will offer to give you the key needed to decrypt your files once they have been paid. Searching the Internet, you'll find a lot of numbers on the percentage of companies that get their data back after a ransomware attack after paying the ransom. The numbers are so inconsistent that I won't reference any of them, but I will say the probability isn't great. With that bit of wisdom, the best plan is to not fall victim in the first place.

How does the ransomware get into your network? Did someone's credentials get compromised? Did they exploit a hardware vulnerability? While those are all plausible, it's usually a much simpler scenario. It often starts with another one of our attacks from the overview—the phishing attack. That's right. The ransomware probably made its way into your network by an employee clicking on a link in an email, which installed the software. Humans are fallible and things will happen, but it happens too often.

So, if it's often caused by human error, how can you prevent it? There are several steps you can take to reduce the likelihood of a successful ransomware attack. Some are technical, and some are training and behavior modification. Here are some of the common prevention methods:

- **Maintain regular backups.** The most crucial defense against ransomware is to maintain regular backups of your data. Ensure that backups are performed on a separate and isolated system, network, or cloud storage. This will allow you to restore your data without paying the ransom in case of an attack.
- **Test backup restores.** Backups are useless if they can't be restored. A regular schedule should be devised to test restoring those backups. Finding problems during restore testing is better than discovering them during an actual breach.
- **Keep software up to date.** Regularly update your operating system, antivirus software, and other applications to the latest versions. Software updates often include patches that address known vulnerabilities, making it harder for ransomware to exploit them.
- **Use security software.** Install reputable antivirus and anti-malware software on all devices and keep them up-to-date. These tools can detect and prevent ransomware infections.
- **Be cautious with email attachments and links.** Ransomware is often delivered through phishing emails containing malicious attachments or links. Avoid clicking on suspicious links and hover over them to verify the URL before clicking. The link you see printed in the email may not be the same as the actual URL behind the scenes.
- **Enable pop-up blockers.** Configure your web browser to block pop-ups and avoid clicking on any pop-up windows that may appear while browsing. These pop-ups often contain malicious code or trigger automatic downloads.
- **Don't download files from untrusted sources.** Only download files and software from reputable sources. Avoid downloading from unverified websites or unknown sources, as they may distribute malware.
- **Use strong, unique passwords.** Ensure that all your online accounts and devices have strong, unique passwords. Use a combination of letters, numbers, and special characters. Additionally, consider using a password manager to securely store and generate strong passwords.
- **Segment your network.** If you're running a business, consider segmenting your network into separate subnetworks. This practice limits the spread of ran-

somware in case one device or segment gets infected. If you're a small business, this may not be possible, but for larger organizations, it should be considered.

- **Educate and train users.** Talk to your employees about the risks of ransomware and how to identify and respond to potential threats. Provide training on safe browsing habits, email security, and the importance of not clicking on suspicious links or opening unknown attachments.

- **Test your training.** Set up or outsource a phishing campaign to test whether your employees are learning enough from the training. If an employee clicks on a link in the email from the phishing campaign, then it will take them to some additional training. This campaign also keeps count of how many attempts were successful so you can determine if a new strategy is needed.

- **Seek outside help.** If you don't have the resources in-house to handle all these things, then find a reputable service provider. They can give you an honest evaluation of your current infrastructure, provide penetration testing, or even manage all your security services.

Conclusion

As long as it's profitable to be a hacker or scammer, these criminals aren't going away. The days of hacking for education and fun are behind us, and it has developed into a billion-dollar industry. Yes, I referred to it as an industry. Illegal but fully formed organizations back much of the hacking today. There are many steps you can take to improve your security posture, but the most important improvement still revolves around training and behavior modification of your employees. I consider employees to be a company's most valuable assets, but they are human and make mistakes. Giving them a solid understanding of how not to be a victim is the best investment you can make. There is also no shame in asking for help. If you don't have the resources and knowledge to implement a secure network, then reach out to a reputable vendor.

About Pervez

Pervez Delawalla has been working in the technology sector since 1991. His talent was recognized early, and he began consulting right out of high school. His early work focused on implementing and managing networks. These were the early days of the Internet, and networks were the main form of security. After seven years of consulting, he formed his first company, Net2EZ, which focused on co-location and data center solutions. He landed his first big contract with Myspace, where his company was responsible for managing all the behind-the-scenes hosting operations. Net2EZ continued to grow under his leadership and went on to manage seven data centers and hosted some very large multinational corporations. He decided to sell the company in 2016 and look for a new challenge.

In 2017, Pervez started VegaNext. VegaNext is a managed services provider, but more specifically, a managed security services provider, where security is at the forefront of their offerings. Within just a couple of months of starting VegaNext, they landed some large contracts, which they still have today. They currently have fifty-plus clients on their roster. Pervez likes to refer to them as partners rather than clients or customers. He sees the relationship as one where they rely on each other to be successful. At VegaNext, they treat every partner's network as if it were their own, and they see an attack on a partner's network as an attack on them.

When not busy keeping his clients safe from the bad guys, you can find Pervez spending quality time with his wife and two sons. When his schedule permits, he likes to spend time on the course playing golf or on the court playing basketball. Pervez also has a passion for flying and is working on getting his private pilot license.

For more information, contact Pervez at VegaNext:

Email: pervez@VegaNext.com
Phone: (888) 834-2550
Web: www.VegaNext.com

Chapter 4

WHY CYBERSECURITY IS NOT ONE-AND-DONE

Matt Horning

E very business needs to have good cybersecurity practices. This isn't news to anyone, yet I'm constantly surprised by the number of companies that have little to no cybersecurity in place. Even those that implement security policies and practices rarely keep them updated to match the latest threats. Like a car, your cybersecurity requires maintenance and sometimes a new model. Your cybersecurity must evolve as the criminals evolve. I promise you, the criminals are very creative and are constantly devising new ways to get past your defenses.

A Brief History of Cybersecurity—Innocent Beginnings

The year is 1971. The first computer virus, Creeper, was created. This program targeted mainframe computers and moved across the network outputting "I'M THE CREEPER: CATCH ME IF YOU CAN." In response, Reaper, the first antivirus program, was created in 1972. The Reaper program just deleted the Creeper by following it across the network.[11] Although this was an innocent game of cat and mouse, you will learn how quickly that innocence was lost. Most of the early computer breaches were by insiders reading and stealing information they weren't authorized to access. It didn't take long for cyberattacks to graduate from educational to malicious. In 1986, a German hacker gained access to Pentagon computers. His plan was to sell the data to Russian KGB operatives. That led to the weaponization of computer viruses by governments and criminals.[12]

The Modern Cybersecurity Landscape—Innocent to Weaponized

Today, cyberattacks target individuals, businesses, and governments daily. Cybercrime is estimated to cost the world close to $10.5 trillion a year by 2025.[13] Hacking in the early days was often the work of individuals. These days, hacking has become organized. Today, there are state-sponsored hackers, organized crime gangs, and terrorist groups that all want your data and money. Since many of these organizations aren't in the United States, it is increasingly difficult to find them, and if we do find them, it's nearly impossible to prosecute them or recover any stolen data or money. In 2020, the FBI received over two thousand Internet-crime complaints *per day*, and those are just the ones that were reported.[14]

Modern Cyberthreats

There are thousands of cyberthreats today. I'll touch on some of the most common threat categories businesses should be prepared for. These threats include malware, ransomware, and payment redirection.

"Malware" is a broad term for a malicious program covertly installed on a computer system. Hackers use malware as an entry point into your network. Once they get a foothold on your computer, they work their way outward, infecting other devices on your network. They then will investigate and collect intelligence on your business and users to find out the best way to wage an attack and maximize profit. The #1 way malware gets installed is through social engineering with a process called phishing (pronounced "fishing"). Phishing involves sending unsolicited emails, known as spam, hoping someone will click on a link that will install malware on their computer.

If you watch the news or have read a paper in the last few years, you've undoubtedly heard of ransomware. Hackers use ransomware to encrypt your data and demand payment to provide you with the key needed to decrypt your files. You would think you could recover by restoring backups, but the hackers attempt to encrypt your backups as well. There is no guarantee that the hackers will release your file, even if you pay the ransom. And now the cybercriminals are going to your customers and vendors, demanding an additional ransom payment so the hackers will not release these companies' information on the dark web. This, of course, affects your relationship with those companies, but it also hurts your reputation in ways you may never recover from. And to top that off, the United States government is looking to criminally charge businesses that pay the ransom because they are funding terrorism.

Finally, let's talk about payment redirection and how effective it is at stealing money from your business. Payment redirection often succeeds through the social engineering of your employees. The cybercriminals send a fake email, known as spoofing, to someone in your company. This fictitious email will include an invoice for payment, which may be valid, but it includes a payment link that is NOT valid. Most cyber protection will not stop these types of attacks. The best way to fight a low-tech attack is with a low-tech solution. Educate your users about cyberthreats and train them to simply call the sender to confirm that they have changed their payment options. Do not ask by replying to the email. That is not enough. Pick up the phone and call the contact who is documented in your existing CRM system. Hackers will try to trick you into contacting *them* instead of the customer.

How to Protect Your Business—Onions?

Now that you know some of the common attacks, how do you protect yourself against them? As the title implies—you can't just set it and forget it. The number, type, and sophistication of cyberattacks are constantly improving, and your cybersecurity practices must keep up and, ideally, stay one step ahead. This requires your cybersecurity needs to be implemented in layers. You get it—just like an onion. The first layer you need to think about is you and your employees—the least secure layer and the hardest to control within your business. A Verizon report on data breaches estimated that 82% of breaches are a result of human error.[15] It used to be sufficient to have a cyber-training event that you and your employees could attend. Now that cybercriminals are so creative and relentless, you need to take the same approach and be relentless as well. Your business and your employees' jobs depend on everyone understanding that cybercrime is real and that you are targets, no matter the size of your business. A 2022 survey found that 75% of SMBs could not continue operating if they were victims of a ransomware attack.[16]

The next layer you need to think about is the perimeter. In the old days (prior to 2020), this was easy to understand. Put in a good firewall that does packet scanning and you are good. Now, with so many work-from-home options, the perimeter is gone. How do you protect employees who work on networks about which you have no knowledge or control? This is where the new term "zero trust" comes in. In short, you and your IT partner will treat each computer as its own office and control all traffic coming from and going to that computer. You accomplish this with a VPN (virtual private network). This allows all traffic to be controlled, no matter where the employee works. It is quickly becoming the new normal on how to manage and protect businesses from threats that employees can find on unknown and untrusted networks.

The third layer we are going to talk about is the software on the computers, phones, and tablets that you or your employees own. Moving forward, all computer equipment needs to be owned by the business. I am not going to dive into that discussion here, but trust me, you need to move in that direction. Bring-your-own-device laptops need to be in your past. We need to implement this third layer through a combination of antivirus, managed detection and response, endpoint detection and response, elevation control, and only allowing approved software on company computers. Cybercriminals are too creative, move too quickly, and are too many in number for an "antivirus" software to suffice. Yes, you need it, but it is one little layer on your computer. The real power is in auditing software and ONLY installing software that is approved for the work function of the employee. Once you do that, you can really lock down the computer and allow the security software to show its power. Businesses shy away from elevation control (forcing employees to engage with the IT provider before installing new software or updates) because they simply have too many programs that the employee needs, and it creates complexity and noise that frustrates the employer and the employees. Once this layer is tuned, it can be extremely effective and rewarding for the employees.

The last layer is to protect your software-as-a-service applications. SaaS applications such as Office 365, Salesforce, and QuickBooks Online are quickly changing how we do business. You may ask, "I pay for these products—don't they provide security?" Well, it's complicated. Most provide basic security, which may not be enough for your business or your cyber insurance company. This means you need to understand what is being provided and what risks you need to take responsibility for so you can be confident you are covered.

Things to think about for your SaaS are:

- **SPAM protection.** Is the basic protection enough for my business, or do I need something with more features?
- **Backups.** Does my SaaS application provide backups? Does it meet my business practices and regulatory requirements?

- **Alerts.** Does the SaaS product alert you or your IT provider if something has gone wrong?
- **Access control.** Does it force your employees to use multifactor authentication (MFA)?

Conclusion

Folks, this is serious stuff. When you look at the numbers, cybercrime is estimated to cost the world close to $10.5 trillion a year by 2025.[17] With numbers like that, we all need to pay attention. Think of it like this: If that was a nation-state GDP, it would be the third-largest economy in the world. We need to think differently, and we need to snap out of our slumber. We are watching the largest transfer of wealth in the world, and that transfer is going to the criminals.

Even if you think you've done your due diligence by implementing some security protocols, you can't just set things on autopilot and move on to the next thing. Cybersecurity requires ongoing maintenance and planning, or you run a significant chance of closing the doors to your business forever. If you think your business is too small to be a target—you're wrong! Small to medium-sized businesses are targets because hackers know they frequently lack the cybersecurity resources of larger corporations. And if your SMB is hacked, many of you don't have the funds to survive longer than six months after the attack.[18] If you don't have the in-house expertise, consider outsourcing your IT support to a firm that is cybersecurity-focused.

If you want to be responsible for your own cybersecurity, then take some steps to stay informed by signing up for cybersecurity bulletins and alerts from trusted sources. Some sources I consider trustworthy are *Krebs On Security* (www.krebsonsecurity.com), *Hacker News* (www.thehackernews.com), and *Bleeping Computer* (www.bleepingcomputer.com). Also, sign up for support notices and alerts from your software and hardware vendors so you are in the know. Keep yourself and your employees trained on how to spot social engineering attacks and keep your antivirus protections up-to-date. In this modern age of constant hacks, it can seem overwhelming to keep up, but if you plan and stay informed, then you can give yourself a fighting chance at avoiding a major hack.

About Matt

Matt Horning, along with his wife, Isadora, are co-owners of Blue Tree Technology, a full-service technology solution provider that focuses on the technology needs of small to medium-sized businesses in and around the Kansas City, Missouri, area. They provide managed IT services, networking, security, and co-managed IT services.

Matt points to the core values of Blue Tree Technology and readily admits they are not the IT provider for everyone. They spend time finding clients who align with their mission of "class-leading, security-focused IT support" and their core values. "Our support needs to be a win-win-win," he says. "A win for the Blue Tree Technology company. A win for the client company. And finally, a win for the staff of both organizations. If we can find the triple win, everyone is happy, and we can expect the relationship to last for years. We enjoy long-term clients, and we strive to acquire them."

After graduating high school in 1990, Matt went to college to appease his mom but quickly realized it wasn't for him. He worked odd jobs to pay the bills but hadn't found his calling. In the late '90s, he was presented with an opportunity to work with an IT company installing desktop computers in a local school district. Matt really enjoyed the job, especially seeing how excited students and teachers were about technology. He picked up that enthusiasm for technology and knew he had found his calling.

He next moved on to the corporate world of IT, initially as a network administrator, where he honed his skills and soaked up as much knowledge as possible. After working a couple corporate jobs, he knew it wasn't the environment he wanted to be in. Matt had never cared for the politics of corporate life and will admit that he struggled to keep his opinions to himself, which didn't always go over well.

In the early 2000s, Matt decided it was time to take the knowledge he had accumulated and start his own business. He had a client willing to write a letter espousing his skills and business acumen, and he sent it out to 500 local businesses. Within two months, Matt had more business than he was prepared for. He ran that company for fifteen years until he bought a business named Velocity Computer Tech, which came with employees and a storefront. Just before the pandemic, Matt had the opportunity to purchase an IT support company called KC Computer Support, which complemented the existing services they offered. As part of the merger, they rebranded to Blue Tree Technology.

For more information, contact Matt at Blue Tree Technology:

    Email: hello@bluetreetechnology.com
    Phone: (816) 256-2595
    Web: www.bluetreetechnology.com

Chapter 5

HOW TO TAKE THE CONFUSION OUT OF COMPLIANCE
Ron Shoe

For ten long years, war raged between the Greeks and Trojans over the abduction of Helen, the beautiful wife of Spartan king Menelaus, by Paris of Troy. The Greeks tried everything to break through Troy's formidable walls, with no luck.

And then Odysseus had an idea . . .

What if they built a huge wooden horse, stuffed it with soldiers, and left it outside the city gates?

Pretending to admit defeat, the Greeks left the giant horse behind and sailed home. Thinking the horse was a victory trophy, the Trojans joyfully hauled it inside their city. But later that night, while the Trojans were sleeping off the celebrations of their supposed triumph, Greek soldiers popped out of the horse and overran the city.

It makes one wonder—was Odysseus the world's first hacker? Indeed, the term "Trojan horse" has since become widely known as a strategy used by cybercriminals to snake their way inside your network to do you and your business harm.

Clearly, Troy's citizens failed to understand the risk they were taking in accepting this "gift" dropped on their doorstep. It must have been a truly puzzling situation—who would've expected that their archenemies would simply abandon their siege, turn tail, and head for the hills . . . while leaving behind this amazing GIFT?

City management simply didn't have any policies in place to deal with this sort of thing.

I'm glad this ancient legend remains part of our common language because it provides an easy-to-grasp way of understanding a very real modern danger—*cybersecurity*—especially given that so much content on that topic is a muddle of complexity and technobabble.

Cybersecurity and Compliance Aren't All That Complex

Honestly, if I were starting from scratch and trying to figure out what matters most in keeping my business safe and secure from cybercriminals, after a few minutes of seeing what's out there, I'd rather be rubbing sand in my eyes.

It's ridiculous, even tragic, that we can't do better—because small and medium-sized businesses all over the world are increasingly getting hammered by cybercrime. The risks from Trojan horses and other threats aren't declining; in fact, they're getting worse.

Helping the little guy stay safe is why I'm so passionate about doing something different to cut through the confusion. This book is just one of many things I'm doing (videos, articles, haikus, and parody songs) that are designed to be entertaining enough to help people want to pay attention and inadvertently learn things that make them and their businesses safer from cybercrime.

Let's start with the fact that so many people confuse the terms "cybersecurity" and "compliance." Actually, the distinction between the two is simple:

- *Cybersecurity* is "Oh crap, Russia's hacking my network. How do I stop them?"
- *Compliance* is the Department of Justice or FBI showing up, saying, "Hey, six months ago, Russia broke in and stole stuff from your network. To prove you weren't negligent, show us documented proof that you were doing all the things to be compliant you said you were doing back then."

Not so hard to get, is it? And by taking the steps necessary to put your company into *compliance*, you're solving the *cybersecurity* challenge at the same time.

Now, to me, this boils down to three simple rules:

RULE #1—Get Buy-in from the Executive Team

The biggest obstacle most companies face regarding compliance is its acceptance as a necessity by the CEO and the executive team.

Reluctance is natural—I'll wager that when that giant horse showed up, the first one out the gate to welcome it in was Troy's king.

Of course, he should've known better. But the fact of the matter was that he and his "trusted" band of advisors failed to take the risk seriously, and they didn't have any policies in place to deal with the unexpected.

It's super-critical for us to have the complete buy-in of senior management along with ownership. Because compliance isn't something you "sort of" do. It represents both a shift in mindset as well as an all-out commitment moving forward.

If you don't have this kind of acceptance starting at the very top of the organization, there's no way it will ever happen. In fact, it can't.

For example, we had a client who, even though they paid lip service to most of the things we told them regarding security, hesitated when we asked them to do things like turning on multifactor authentication (MFA), using a password manager to store and encrypt passwords, and to stop sharing passwords across different services.

We practically had to beg them to "PLEASE stop making passwords that are so easy to remember."

(By the way, here's a good rule of thumb for you: if you can remember a password, it's a bad password.)

They were using the same password for everything: **Alabama7**. And they didn't want to utilize any of the other tools and protections.

Well, their credentials got hacked and republished on the dark web, and within twenty-four hours, their email was compromised.

Fortunately, our security team was ready and prevented further damage, but the client was required to send embarrassing notifications to all their customers because that's what the law says.

(By the way, they let us put in MFA and those other changes pronto.)

RULE #2—Get Buy-in from the Employees

I get it. Getting employees to implement these kinds of protections can be a hard sell. The citizens of Troy fatally assumed that the walls of the city would keep them safe. They were in utter denial about the looming threat and blissfully went on with their daily duties . . . until it was too late.

But if Troy had instead prepared a documented security plan, and every citizen had been involved in it and trained on it, someone just might have recognized the Greeks' wooden malware and saved the day.

And they didn't have to make this training boring.

They could have had "Screw Achilles" theme parties where they ate Trojan pizza and educated the citizens on the latest tactics of those sneaky Greeks. Their bards could have written lyre songs lampooning the enemy and teaching Trojans not to trust Greeks and how to recognize them.

With just a tiny bit of creativity, they could have trained each citizen on what to do if (when?) the walls were breached and how to respond properly in a crisis.

During World War II, every American did their part to contribute to the war effort. Remember Rosie the Riveter? Today is no different. We are literally in a cyber-war right now, and the way you can do your part is by learning how to make yourself safer from cybercrime and teaching your employees how they can help. We are all in this together.

Honestly, in the past, compliance and cybersecurity always meant taking things away and making life for employees more complicated: "Sorry, it used to be two clicks, now it's three clicks, and you've got to pull out your phone for every single job function."

But now, thanks to improvements in technology and better training, we can make it a lot easier for anyone to keep their identity (and their data) safe. One thing that really excites me is the fact that putting these safety measures in place is getting easier for our users to do—and to do so cost-effectively.

This involves things like (non-boring) user training, password hygiene, MFA, and other tools, such as single sign-on (SSO) user authentication, which enables users to access multiple applications and services securely with just one set of credentials.

But the bottom line is that even with tools and training, your employees still need to DO the things we tell them to do. This means sometimes you have to tell employees that, even if they don't want to use MFA or strong passwords, they HAVE to do these things because, otherwise, they're potentially going to be the one who brings down the whole business.

RULE #3—Engage the Professionals

How do you take the confusion out of your health? You engage a doctor.

How do you take the confusion out of the law? You engage a lawyer.

And where the Greeks and Trojans consulted the oracles and invoked Athena and Ares, their gods of wisdom and war, you should consult and work with folks who know what they're doing. (I'll stop short of calling us oracles.)

Never underestimate the enemy because they are good. You're outclassed—which is why these laws exist in the first place.

Fortunately, if you just do the things prescribed by your compliance framework (HIPAA, FTC Safeguards, etc.), cybersecurity will take care of itself. Just do what the law says. If you're not an expert in doing what the law says, hire someone who is.

Implementing compliance is much like the process Troy underwent through its founding. In the beginning, there were no defenses whatsoever, only homes. But after a few devastating attacks and losses, they decided that protecting themselves was a worthy pursuit.

First off, they set about building a wall around the city. The initial iteration of the wall was the least impressive—just piles of stacked rocks—but they had to start somewhere.

Then they built a tower. Then they expanded the rock wall. Then they dug the wall down to bedrock. Then they started replacing those stacks of rocks with carefully hewn stones that fit together more tightly. Then they built watchtowers on the corners. Then they reinforced the gate.

They kept building and refining until, eventually, they'd established a citadel of protection for their people.

Building that wall took the Trojans a lot of time and cost them a LOT of money, but it was worth it. They NEVER stopped building and reinforcing, and eventually the wall was so massive that the Greeks marveled that it must have been built by the gods Apollo and Poseidon themselves.

That wall kept Troy safe for a very long time until the Greeks used some wily skullduggery to get around it.

Compliance is similar to how Troy evolved *their* defenses. You're constantly making changes and improving things. Fortunately, you don't have to wing it like the Trojans did because all compliance frameworks mandate a ***process*** to follow:

- You must have a security plan;
- You must do an assessment that identifies the things you're not doing that you should;
- And you just keep working through that process, those items, over time.

Safeguarding your IDENTITY is ultimately what this comes down to. There are roughly thirty BILLION devices on the Internet today that aren't yours. We have to know for sure that it's YOU who is accessing your data.

Although fewer people now deny that cybercrime exists or that it's ever going to happen to them, cybersecurity solutions, unfortunately, are not cheap. It's an expensive cost of doing business that literally did not exist years ago.

It's a game you have to play, but you need to know and understand whom you are facing.

Imagine for a moment that you're Troy and you're in a war. But instead of the Greeks with horses, bronze weapons, and arrows, you're fighting a World War II army. They have steel, internal combustion engines, gunpowder, tanks, mortars, rockets, howitzers, and airplanes.

That wouldn't be much of a battle, would it? That's what their team looks like—nation-states like China and Russia and global crime syndicates with organizations as mature as a Fortune 100 company. So, what does your team look like?

Be honest . . .

If it's just you, you're going to get squashed under the proverbial Panzer tank.

You need professionals on your team because they've got professionals on theirs.

Just Get Started

Troy's downfall could've turned out differently. What if they had:

- Put in place a compliance framework with policies on how to accept Greek gifts during wartime?
- Created a plan for dealing with unexpected "surprises" from unknown entities?
- Established procedures and systems to ensure everyday citizens didn't get easily suckered in by something that looked cool?

We'll never know whether they could have avoided that Bronze Age ransomware and the devastation it ultimately caused.

But we CAN resolve to not let that hard lesson learned fade into the dust of history.

Do SOMETHING. Just get started.

A common misconception about compliance is that it's all or nothing. It's black or white. Not true. It's about progress, not perfection. You must be compliant with the process and execute it in good faith.

So, maybe you're thinking, *We've done that assessment and there are forty-three things we're not doing. We can't do forty-three things. We don't have the money, time, resources, whatever!*

I get it. So, pick out the three things you can do this year—the things that will have the most impact. Then do those three things. And then next year, you repeat the assessment, which shows you've passed those three things. Now, you're only down to forty things that need to get done.

That's how it goes. You demonstrate that you understand the problem, you're using the right process, and you're taking it seriously. You're making a list, checking it twice, and knocking things off in the order that you're best able to accomplish according to the standards.

It's really not that complicated. And if you do need help along the way, making compliance and cybersecurity easier is key to our company's mission.

About Ron

Ron Shoe and his business partner, Frank Moles, founded SIP Oasis in 2007 to serve the needs of customers in Birmingham, Alabama, and beyond and to give clients what they so desperately needed but struggled to find—someone who could FINALLY make IT and telecom EASY.

SIP Oasis provides white-glove technology and security services with top-line solutions engineered to help small and midsize companies meet business goals while managing costs.

Every business they serve—whether it's a car dealership, financial planner, mortgage company, or multifamily complex, to name a few—first and foremost wants their technology to work. That was what they were promised when they signed up for service. And when it doesn't work, they want ONE phone number to call, which had better be answered by someone who CAN and genuinely WANTS to help.

For whatever reason, when it comes to working with the managed services industry, it always seems to be the other guy's problem. The Internet provider blames the router, the network guy blames the Internet, the phone guy blames the carrier, the carrier blames the phone system . . .

SIP Oasis takes responsibility and accountability for ALL OF IT because you should only have one throat to choke. You want your technology to work FOR your business, and you only want to have to make one call to fix things if it doesn't.

You can count on SIP Oasis to support your network infrastructure, Internet services, Wi-Fi, mobile phones, email, storage, security, disaster recovery, and applications—all via ONE RELATIONSHIP.

Plus, they'll work with you in a way that's both fun and free of all the jargon and computer-speak. Ron is passionate about getting the message out about compliance and security in ways that cut through the oppressive techno-fog—with crazy content, videos, haikus, songs . . . whatever it takes. (They've even released their own craft beer, named "Breached Blonde Ale.")

Known as the "Weird Al Yankovic of Cybersecurity," Ron is a guitarist and musician and has written a number of songs about keeping your business safe from hackers. He met his wife, Kristin, in college, and they now have two grown kids. Along with music, they love to travel.

Ron graduated in 1992 from Furman University with a Bachelor of Arts in history. He also attended Indiana University Bloomington in 1991 for Russian language immersion and lived in Russia during the summers of 1992 and 1993.

Specialties include:

- Network Management
- Managed Security
- Security Operations Center (SOC)
- IT Help Desk
- CIO
- Dark Web Monitoring
- Managed HIPAA Compliance
- Managed FTC Safeguards Compliance
- VoIP
- Telecommunications
- Cloud Services
- Microsoft 365
- Unified Communications
- Customer Service
- Call Centers
- Systems Integration
- Hosted PBX
- SIP Trunking

For more information, contact Ron and SIP Oasis:

Email: help@sipoasis.com
Phone: (205) 623-1200
Web: www.sipoasis.com

Chapter 6

THE PERCEPTIONS ABOUT COMPLIANCE THAT COULD PUT YOUR BUSINESS IN DANGER
Gino Capito and Ray Riddle

W hy should your business worry about compliance at all?

Do you think you're already safe or too small to be a target?

Do you think you can work under the compliance table and beg forgiveness later from a compliance auditor?

Perceptions like these put businesses in danger, and not just your own. Your suppliers, customers, and everyone else your business touches can also be affected.

Whenever a business, large or small, gets breached, people want to know if the business did everything they could to protect their information. This isn't just the victims. Your cyber insurance provider will also want to know—so might the credit agencies and even the government.

The entire compliance industry came about because businesses made promises about security and data protection they couldn't keep. What will you say to regulators after a criminal has attacked you?

Will you be able to show that you were compliant, had a plan of action, and shut down the attack quickly? Or will it get exposed that your compliance wasn't up to par and you left your company vulnerable?

Did you know that over 230,000 new pieces of malware are produced daily? Attacks are always evolving, and it's impossible to achieve perfect security, but

41

compliance with best practices is the best way to show you've done your due diligence. It also makes it far harder for you to get breached and far easier to detect breaches.

Yet many of our new clients have some persistent perceptions about compliance that put their businesses in danger. Let's knock these out of the way and show why clinging to these ideas could put your business in danger.

"Is My Business Really Required to Comply?"

Business owners, particularly owners of small to medium-sized businesses, frequently wonder if they are "really" required to comply. Many are completely unaware that there are compliance requirements for their industry or demographic niche.

Complying with cybersecurity regulations seems disruptive and can be overwhelming. Even knowing which regulations apply to your business and where to begin working toward compliance causes some business owners to struggle.

It's understandable since there are so many programs, and they seem aimed at companies much larger than a small business. However, you're still required to comply with regulations specific to your industry and the markets you serve, no matter the size of your business.

Here's a quick checklist to see if you need to comply with at least one of the most common regulations. Ask yourself if your business does any of the following:

- Do you work in medicine or have access to protected health information?
- Do you sell vehicles, cash checks, or work in finance, real estate, taxes, or post-secondary education and receive Title IV funding?
- Do you work with any kind of controlled unclassified information from the government or deeper levels of government security?
- Do you work with customers in the European Union?
- Do you accept, process, store, or transmit ANY kind of credit card information?

If you answered yes to any of these, then there is at least one compliance program you should follow. If you're not sure which regulations you need to follow, we encourage you to speak with a compliance professional. You need to learn which compliance regulations you must follow and how to get compliant.

We encourage all businesses to work toward PCI-DSS compliance as a basic measure to protect against credit information theft and fraud. Most businesses handle credit card information, so this is a good first certification to aim for.

"I'm Too Small to Be a Target"

Small businesses, especially sole proprietors and partnerships, often believe their risk of falling victim to cybercrime is low. This is absolutely false. Nearly 43% of all cyberattacks are aimed at small businesses, and only 15% of SMBs have good cyber hygiene.

Justin Weller, director of business development at Blackpoint Cyber, is fond of saying, "You are not too small to be hacked; you are just too small to be on the news." Every business is a potential target, even if you're a sole proprietor.

In fact, successful sole proprietors make for attractive targets, especially if they have high-value data. Lawyers are particularly at risk. They have lots of personal information that their clients would prefer to keep under wraps. One breach would destroy a lawyer's reputation as a guardian of their client's secrets.

Whether it is due to believing their size makes them an unattractive target or to a lack of staff resources to focus on compliance and cybersecurity issues, many small businesses struggle to address the vulnerabilities inherent in computers and networks.

So, how do you prepare yourself to get compliant? If your business does not have the expertise or capacity to work through compliance preparation and documentation, you should partner with a company to assist you through the process. By partnering with a company that specializes in compliance and cybersecurity, you'll know you are spending your efforts on the right things to meet current best practices.

Also, general business insurers are requiring businesses to carry cyber insurance, even for smaller businesses. Meeting compliance standards could help you get more cost-effective cyber insurance and business insurance. Vice versa, many insurers are also requiring compliance verification and will deny claims if you haven't met their standards!

Once you comply with the regulatory burden, you have created a potential difference between you and some of your competitors. Your compliance is indicative that your organization is following best practices for your industry. Similar to being bonded and insured, compliance builds trust with potential customers.

Finally, compliance programs will give your business a road map of what to do if you ever get breached. Guidance on how to notify your customers of a breach and what to do afterward will help you continue operations with as little disruption as possible.

"Compliance Will Prevent Me from Doing Business"

Another perception we see is that doing the work to get compliant will put a business at a competitive disadvantage. If only they didn't have to follow regulations, their operations would be more agile and less expensive. They see it as business prevention instead of business protection. This is a dangerous mindset.

Consider that 60% of all SMBs that get breached go out of business within six months. Why is that? First, it's incredibly expensive if you've been breached. Even a simple ransomware attack that doesn't steal your data costs businesses an average of $133,000 to restore operations.

The costs skyrocket if records are lost or stolen. Here are some statistics about such costs:

- The average cost of a lost or stolen data record involving personally identifiable information (PII) is $176 per record.
- The average cost of a data breach is $3.86 million. For companies with over 50,000 records, the average cost is $6.3 million.
- Each attack involving a compromised password against an SMB costs an average of $384,598.

Consider also that it takes an average of sixty-nine days to contain a breach. Each day, you may face fines from regulators if your PII, financial data, or similar data aren't protected according to regulations. By the time a cybercriminal is detected and you've finished paying for the incident response, it's no wonder most businesses don't survive.

On the other hand, if you have a compliance strategy that meets the standards, you experience several advantages if you're breached. First, it will be much harder to get breached. Second, compliance strategies have procedures regarding protecting data and notifying customers after a breach is detected. These can help reduce reputational impacts.

You'll also avoid the hefty fines for noncompliance that governments can levy on businesses. Also, if you get sued for the data breach, showing compliance with all current regulations will reduce your legal liability.

Compliance with regulations is not simple and is not a one-time thing. Once you get certified, you still have to identify and eliminate risks and monitor and manage compliance. Standards get updated with time, and attacks are always growing.

Compliance requires developing processes, practices, training, and monitoring to ensure your business is protected and resilient. If companies don't spend the effort to get compliant, then they are putting their business at risk.

Yes, all of this will cost money as well. But the cost of a breach will far outweigh the cost of working with a compliance expert and implementing a strong compliance strategy. Plus, if you are compliant and a noncompliant competitor gets breached, you're in a prime position. You can leverage your compliance status to grab their market share.

"Compliance Is Not My Problem"

Compliance is not just a matter for your IT team. It also involves management, the C-suite, HR, and other teams. Compliance provides a framework so IT and operations can work together to protect the company's ability to generate revenue.

We see instances where token efforts at compliance are seen as enough. We also see many companies leaning too heavily on software, believing that makes them compliant. Some even go so far as to say that cyber insurance will cover any costs, so they don't have to do the work of compliance.

It is important to understand that this isn't enough to help you if the regulators come knocking. You own the business, so you're the accountable party if the job isn't done correctly. Even if you think your policies and procedures are compliant, you won't know for sure until you get them checked by a third party.

In fact, many regulations, such as CMMC, are moving toward third-party auditing of strategies to get and keep the certification. That's why engaging with MSPs that have a compliance verification service is becoming more popular.

"Once I'm Compliant, I'm Safe"

Remember that compliance and security are two different things.

Once you get compliant with regulations, you've taken a major step toward protecting your business. But it's only one step in the right direction. Compliance is not a one-time event, nor does it remove the possibility of human errors compromising your security.

Attacks change all the time. Regulations change all the time. Your business also changes all the time. Any change could create a situation where you need to improve your security or update your compliance strategy to reflect new policies, procedures, or work processes.

It's Never Too Late to Start

If you've noticed you've fallen into one of these traps about compliance, take heart. It is never too late to move toward compliance. Even if you got audited before you're certified, showing you were actively taking steps in the right direction will help you.

Denying that you need to get compliant or getting angry about the regulations won't help you. The way to move forward if you know you're not compliant is to work with an expert. If you already have a managed services security provider helping you with security, find out if they also handle compliance certification. Many security providers, including our own, offer this service.

Complying with data protection and cybersecurity requirements isn't just about making regulators happy and avoiding fines. There are other significant advantages:

- Clients are more likely to trust your company and close deals because they know you're taking steps to protect their data.
- If a competitor gets breached, you can leverage your compliance standards to draw their clients to you.
- You could get discounts on your cyber insurance or general business insurance for proving compliance.
- If you're the target of an acquisition, proof of compliance will let the potential buyer know they're not walking into a minefield of regulatory and security issues.

Most of all, compliance gives you peace of mind. You'll know your company is doing the right things to protect customer data. You can prove it to whoever wants to know. Compliance also increases the speed of catching criminals and recovering from breaches because everyone will know what to look for and what to do.

We encourage you to see if you need to get compliant with regulations and start working with a team to help you meet these standards. You'll be doing your part to fight against cybercrime.

About Gino and Ray

Gino Capito is the chief technology officer of TeleComp. He oversees the company's internal data and security infrastructure and heads the Software Development and Solution Architects divisions. Prior to co-founding TeleComp, Gino founded Platinum Technologies, a company focused on networking, servers, and Cisco VoIP. Later, after acquiring another company with a business partner, he co-founded TeleComp in 2003.

Ray Riddle is the chief operations officer of TeleComp and the former COO of Beasley Technology. Prior to his position as COO, he worked for major computer manufacturers Sun Microsystems and Data General.

Ray is also the supervisor of Professional Services at TeleComp. This role manages the network engineering, unified communications, carrier services, virtual schools, and project management teams.

TeleComp was founded in 2003 in Northwest Arkansas, a unique entrepreneurial hotspot in the Midwest. Since 2018, the company has expanded deeply into South Central United States to become one of the largest MSPs in the region. Their goal is to provide high-quality, customizable IT solutions with an emphasis on customer service.

For more information, contact Ray or Gino at TeleComp:

Email: ray.riddle@telecomp.com or gino.capito@telecomp.com
Phone: (888) 831-9400 (main office)
Web: www.telecomp.com
LinkedIn: www.linkedin.com/company/telecomp-holdings/

Chapter 7

STOP OVERCOMPLICATING COMPLIANCE BY STARTING WITH THE BASICS
Lisa A. Brown

D id you nearly pass over this chapter as soon as you saw the title? Be honest. I know compliance is not cool and sexy. I wanted to call this chapter "Puppies and Unicorns," but the publisher wouldn't go for it. But since you're already here, let's talk about compliance and why it doesn't have to keep you up at night. I work with clients all over the country and specialize in compliance-driven industries, so I know it can be a little overwhelming. However, we aren't going to focus on a specific compliance mandate but rather on how to tackle it regardless of the compliance regulations you're required to adhere to.

Before I tell you how your business should tackle compliance, I'm going to confess something. I help businesses deal with compliance issues daily, but even I struggled in the past to make it a priority for my business. Now that I've let my guard down, I hope it puts you at ease a bit, knowing that I've also been there—we've all been there. By reading this chapter, you get to benefit from someone who has first-hand experience changing the way companies view compliance.

Every business, big and small, has rules and regulations they must "comply" with. If you deal with health care data, you must comply with the Health Insurance Portability and Accountability Act (HIPAA) regulations. If you are a contractor for the Department of Defense, you must comply with the Cybersecurity Maturity Model

Certification (CMMC) requirements. If you own or run a company, I can guarantee there are several you may have to work with, such as the Gramm-Leach-Bliley Act (GLBA), the National Institute of Standards and Technology (NIST), General Data Protection Regulation (GDPR—EU regulations) and Sarbanes-Oxley (SOX), and if you take credit card payments, you must comply with the Payment Card Industry Data Security Standard (PCI DSS). Even if you are just a small business with a few employees, you have human resources requirements to comply with. Most businesses see compliance as something to deal with when they have time. Unfortunately, that mentality could cost you money in fines or, even worse, it could cost you customers.

Trickle-Down Compliance

Trickle-down compliance is just a way of illustrating that if compliance is taken seriously at the top of the organization, then that commitment will flow down to the rest of the organization. If you own a business or are the CEO of a business, you are at the top of the pyramid, and compliance starts with you. If you don't make compliance a priority, how can you expect your employees, vendors, and contractors to? Sitting at the top of the pyramid also means you'll need to allocate the proper funding and resources for compliance. You need a training plan, someone to lead the efforts, and you'll need to measure and report on progress.

An often overlooked resource to consider is time. Understand that it may take employees more time and attention to ensure compliances are met. Empower them to do so because, ultimately, the risk of not taking it seriously from the top down could mean serious fines or even jail time for YOU.

Creating a Culture of Compliance

What does it look like to have a compliance-focused culture? Much as it sounds: It means compliance needs to be considered a core function of the business. Compliance will be the responsibility of every employee. We also must stop thinking of compliance as a chore that adds no value and takes too much time away from "actual work." Compliance is genuine work and, when done properly, it adds value. Just like everything else, work it into your schedule.

This is all worthless without knowing where to start or how to implement something as overwhelming as a cultural shift. I'm going to provide five principles to follow when implementing your compliance overhaul. These principles are a broad approach that will help with any type of compliance within any industry. There are many books that focus on the detailed implementation of a specific type of compliance, but they rarely discuss the idea of a cultural shift or focus on the bigger picture.

The five principles I'm going to focus on include changing your company's mindset about compliance, creating a compliance plan, communicating the plan, measuring your progress, and reviewing and changing the plan as needed. Following these simple guidelines will get you moving toward a culture of compliance.

1. Change the Way You Think About Compliance

It's hard enough to make a personal change, but it's a huge undertaking to change the culture of an entire company, right? It doesn't have to be. Keep it simple. Chip away at the existing perceptions and have open conversations. As the owner, CEO, or leader of a company, you set the tone for others on how you want customers to be treated, how you want your employees to feel appreciated, and the overall culture you want your company to strive for. Changing the way your company views and handles compliance is no different. You set the tone. If you view compliance as a core function of your business operations, then your employees will follow suit. It may not happen overnight, but it will happen.

> *"Not everything that is faced can be changed,*
> *but nothing can be changed until it is faced."*
> —James Baldwin

2. Create a Written Plan

Before you ask—yes, it has to be in writing. Not only will auditors expect a written plan, but it should also be accessible to your employees so they can refer to it as needed. Even if you are a one-person shop, it will help keep you honest if it's written. Ideally, keep this document online and ensure version or source updates are controlled. The plan should include:

- **Identification of which compliances apply to you.** I won't lie—this is going to be the most time-consuming and tedious part of the job. You can assign this task to someone, but I'd prefer you do this one yourself. This will give you an opportunity to really understand all the regulations for your industry or state and what those regulatory agencies are asking of you. Remember, if you are not following the compliance requirements for your state and industry, the blame and fines will fall on you, not your employees. Why not ensure you understand it all from the very beginning!

The easiest way to determine which compliances you need to implement is to reach out to your industry associations and peers. Do not start from scratch or you will get overwhelmed and give up! Ask them for a list of all the regulatory expectations they are currently following. Everyone should have a list, making it easy to reference and follow. You could also reach out to someone like me, your friendly IT provider. Find a provider that specializes in your industry, and they will assist you with compiling everything you will need. Although I work in the technology sector and know firsthand what compliance looks like in my field, we can't forget about all the other areas that may also have compliance requirements. Consider things like HR documents, as well as any financial reporting to the state and federal government.

- **The policies and procedures you need to implement to make sure your vision is achieved.** They need to be clear, concise, and thorough. If you're going to measure against these policies and procedures, employees, clients, and vendors need to understand them. Write them down and share them regularly. Write them in a clear and concise manner, avoiding jargon that could be misunderstood.

- **Information on how your employees can or are expected to contribute.** Your employees are your best resource and biggest risk because, let's face it, they are in the trenches. For regulatory compliances, they must follow the rules. If there is a specific process employees should follow, make sure it is clear. If there are expectations that aren't clear in the policies themselves, they need to be discussed AND resolved. It's also a good idea to let employees know how they can be a part of the conversation, especially with day-to-day tasks. Let me give you an example. An employee left a company laptop in an unlocked car. The laptop was stolen, along with massive amounts of personal patient data. Upwards of four million medical records were exposed, each representing a breach of HIPAA regulations. After the fines were calculated, the company had to pay $5.5 million. A common accident led to one of the largest fines ever levied because of a security breach. Sadly, there are thousands of examples like this, all of which could have been prevented if there had been a clear policy on handling portable devices. One of the many HIPAA compliance regulations we are obligated to follow is protecting personally identifiable information (PII) no matter where it is located.

- **The metrics by which you will measure these policies and procedures for accountability.** This is critical. You should always have a way to measure success and failure. How will the company and employees know if they are doing a good job, and how will you know if they are not?

3. Communicate the Plan

This step is vital for the adoption of the plan and the one that is the most neglected. You cannot expect people to follow the plan if they don't know what it is. Everyone needs to be aware of the plan, but this step is more than just that. This is your opportunity to explain the why, as well as what is expected of everyone. This is also your best opportunity to be an evangelist for compliance. Let your employees, clients, customers, and vendors see that you are intimately involved in creating this plan and that you will be the first to follow it.

This is also a good time to talk to your employees about accountability for not adhering to the included policies and procedures. Remember, they put you at risk every single day. I had a client who almost lost $60,000 in one email. They were trying to purchase a vehicle for their fleet. Emails had been going back and forth about the price, and once they had confirmed that, they were ready to transfer the $60,000 to the seller—via an electronic bank transfer where the account information was in the email. When the client called to inform me, I quickly reacted with a huge NO! Never, ever do a financial transaction where your only confirmation is via an email. Luckily, the client listened to me, contacted the seller via phone, and realized the email communication had been hijacked. It was NOT the correct banking information. A crisis averted—and now there is a policy regarding the transferring of funds.

4. Measuring for Accountability

Setting policies and procedures without a way to measure successes and failures is not a complete plan. You will have clearly defined that everyone is accountable for the successes and failures of each step. We know now that accountability starts with you, but it doesn't end with you. Have an open conversation with your employees about what is working and what is not. If the employees feel the policies and procedures are ambiguous or not clearly defined, then be open to feedback and fix it. If they understand them but still aren't following them, then press for more details, keeping in mind that some are not "optional" but may need to be communicated differently. Don't forget to acknowledge or even celebrate the successes. Making employees feel valued is a simple thing and does wonders for retention.

5. Modify and Repeat

As I alluded to in the previous paragraph, sometimes things need to be adjusted. You should consider the plan to be a living document. Don't just create it and file it away. It needs to be reviewed regularly. The cadence of that review depends on how often things in your industry change. If you are a small company and don't have ties to any heavily regulated industries, then an annual review may be enough. If you are in a heavily regulated sector, then you'll likely need to be more aggressive in scheduling your reviews. You should communicate the plan back to your employees after any major revisions. I would suggest requiring employees to acknowledge that they've read the updated plan. I suggest an annual acknowledgment, even if you haven't made changes. We could all use a refresher sometimes. If you have employees, consider putting someone in charge of this so you can take it off your plate. However, this does not mean you can forget about it. Once again, hold that person accountable and be sure you are diligent in making sure it gets done.

Conclusion

Compliance as a culture doesn't have to be difficult. In fact, it shouldn't be difficult. You need to begin with the basics. A good starting point is changing the way you view and discuss compliance. Research what organizations in your industry are expected or required to do. Create a plan that is manageable and one you can adhere to. Talk to those on the frontline and get input if necessary. Once you have a solid plan, communicate it to the stakeholders. Follow up by creating meaningful metrics against your plan and be sure to track accountability. Remember, this is a living document and will need revision. It all starts at the top. If the owner/CEO embraces compliance, then the rest will follow.

About Lisa

The first thing you notice when talking to Lisa Brown is her passion for business and technology. One of her early clients mistook that passion for being pushy, which led her to coin the slogan *"Passionate, NOT Pushy"* to describe her business. Her love for technology and for her clients is clear, and it shows in the quality of her company's work.

Lisa started CST Group Inc. in 2000, and her husband joined her in 2004. Together, they are an amazing team and balance each other's strengths and weaknesses. With Lisa's background in government and compliance and Shawn's knowledge of networking and security, they have the experience and skills to keep your business running smoothly. CST offers a full catalog of IT services. CST can manage all your IT needs or just the parts you need help with. They offer tailored services such as compliance, networking, security, backup/recovery, and even vendor management.

Lisa and her company have extensive experience working in heavily regulated industries and governments, and they've made a career of helping companies address compliance issues. They've done work in local government, insurance, automotive, legal, and accounting industries—just to name a few. CST Group has helped companies create compliance plans from the ground up, and they also step in to help businesses that just need support to stay on course.

Lisa is a perfectionist when it comes to her clients. She believes that customer service, high service levels, and educating clients make CST a true leader in technology, which has led to their year-over-year growth. If you read the testimonials on their website, you'll see that her customers agree.

For more information, contact Lisa at CST Group Inc.:

Email: lbrown@cstsupport.com
Phone: (877) 954-4100
Web: www.cstsupport.com

Chapter 8

HOW NOT TAKING COMPLIANCE AS A CULTURE SERIOUSLY CAN DESTROY YOUR COMPANY
Chad Brush

"**W**e're a small business. Nobody wants our stuff." I've had more than one person tell me that when I talked to them about compliance and cybersecurity. It's the type of attitude that makes them the perfect target.

Here's a typical example of a potential scenario. Your first employee arrives in the morning, logs into their computer, and gets a screen that says something like, "We want $20,382 by such-and-such date, or we'll delete all your data." Where did they get the $20,382 number? The cyber attackers have rooted around in your network until they found the person with administrator access to QuickBooks (or whatever financial application you use). They know that's how much money you have in the bank for payroll and what you can afford to pay.

Until the situation is rectified, your company will be incapacitated. Operation and commerce come to a halt. Customer orders aren't being filled, and your employees are at a virtual standstill. For some businesses, an extended period of downtime and an unexpected $20,000 ransomware charge could result in them not making payroll and even put them out of business, destroying everything they've built. And the $20,000 figure is low. According to cybersecurity company Sophos, the average ransom payout in 2021 was $812,360.[19]

So, while it may be true that nobody wants your stuff, cyber attackers want your money, and they don't care if they destroy your business to get it. The following are twelve ways not taking compliance seriously can ruin your company:

1. **Your data becomes inaccessible.** Today, *every* company is a *data* company. Gone are the big filing cabinets filled with folders and paper. Hard drives and the cloud have replaced them. Besides containing valuable client information, your data helps you understand your clients better, allows you to make smarter business decisions, and assists you in solving problems and improving your systems and processes. The most devastating result of not taking compliance seriously is that all your information is locked down and you cannot access it. This will grind your business to a halt, which could not only be expensive but could put you out of business permanently.

2. **It will cost you a lot of money.** Data breach costs include costs associated with detection and escalation, post-data breach response, notification of the affected individuals, remediation, public relations, operation disruption and/or destruction, lost intellectual property, lost business, etc. Plus, any legal costs or fines you incur. The average cost of a data breach in the US in 2021 was $4.24 million (IBM and the Ponemon Institute's *2022 Cost of a Data Breach Report*).[20]

   According to IT data protection company Datto, the average cost of downtime across all company sizes is $4,500 a minute (for larger enterprises, the cost is more than $11,600 per minute). Datto also found that one hour of downtime can cost a small business $8,000.[21]

3. **Your reputation could take a big hit.** A company's reputation is directly tied to its success. A company with a solid reputation has good customer loyalty and has no problem attracting new customers and investors. A bad reputation can erode a company's customer base and financial performance. If your business gets hacked, you must report the breach to the applicable state and federal authorities (see #11 for federal reporting information). It can significantly impact your business's reputation if the public becomes aware of it. The press may find out about your company's cybersecurity breach in a few ways. In the name of being transparent with customers, investors, and

the public, the breached company may choose to release the information themselves. If they don't, the press could become aware of it from an insider tip, a third party, or public records and legal filings. News of a cybersecurity breach will spread quickly, and you may find it challenging to attract new customers and hold on to your existing clients. An excellent example of a company whose reputation was damaged by a data breach is Yahoo. They had two separate incidents (2013 and 2014). Personal data was stolen from three billion of their user accounts. Their reputation was severely damaged, and the purchase price when Verizon bought them suffered a $350 million reduction.

4. **Operational disruptions.** How long can your company afford to be down? The length of time a company can be down depends upon the size and industry of the company, the severity of the breach, and how prepared a company is to respond. The longer your company is down, the more money it will cost, the more trust you will lose in the marketplace, and the more your reputation will suffer.

5. **Erosion of employee morale and retention.** Fear, anxiety, and uncertainty are three emotions a breach can instill in your employees, especially if their personal information has been compromised. Decreased job satisfaction and even burnout can result from additional stress and workload. Your employees might even feel embarrassed to work for a company with a severely damaged reputation.

6. **Loss of competitive advantage.** A cybersecurity breach could result in the theft of your intellectual property and trade secrets. If information is stolen about an upcoming merger, acquisition, or new marketing campaign, and it falls into the wrong hands, it could give your competition a leg up in the marketplace. Plus, if you're having legal and financial issues because of your breach, it could distract you from your core business activities, resulting in your business falling behind in the marketplace.

7. **Once the ransom is paid, you become a prime target.** According to Cybereason, a Boston-based cybersecurity software company, 80% of organizations that previously paid a ransom to cyber attackers were exposed to a second attack.[22] They reached this conclusion by surveying 1,263 cybersecurity professionals from the United States, United Kingdom, Spain, Germany, United Arab Emirates, and Singapore. If you're the victim of a cyberattack,

the attacker knows your vulnerabilities and how to exploit them. This is why it's essential to take corrective action immediately. Plus, if you've paid the ransom once, your attacker will assume you'll pay the ransom again.

8. **Higher cybersecurity insurance premiums.** A cybersecurity insurance policy is essential if your business uses technology or collects data. It can cover the costs of a data breach from revenue loss and legal fees for costs associated with recovering stolen data and repairing or replacing compromised computer systems, etc. Buying cybersecurity insurance is like buying life insurance. With life insurance, they ask you questions such as "Are you a smoker?" "What is your height and weight?" "Do you drink alcohol?" "Do you exercise?" and so on. Your monthly payment will be determined by how you answer the questions. One of the first questions an insurance company will ask you about your business when you apply for cybersecurity insurance is "Are you compliant?" Your premiums will be higher if you're not compliant because the risk is greater. They may even decide they don't want you as a customer and refuse to issue a policy. This could hurt your business, as some companies insist their vendors have cybersecurity insurance before dealing with them.

9. **Your cybersecurity insurance could be at risk.** A few years ago, when a business applied for a cybersecurity policy, an insurance company asked you three or four questions. You answered them, paid the premium, and your business moved forward. Because insurance companies have had to pay out a lot of money, those three or four questions have turned into pages and pages. Questions that a typical business might have no idea how to answer accurately. You must provide the insurance company with the correct answers and prove it because if you don't and you have a data breach, and you've marked "Yes" on everything, and they investigate and find out it's not accurate, they will void your policy and you won't receive a payout. A Nashville law firm, which was not my managed services client at the time, was renewing its cybersecurity insurance policy. They called me up and asked me to look at it to ensure they'd filled everything out correctly. They hadn't. They'd marked "Yes" in places where it wasn't true. I explained the ramifications, and they quickly became one of our managed services clients. They now have cybersecurity insurance and are compliant. I can't stress this enough. *It's*

imperative to have someone well-versed in compliance to help you with compliance-related questions.

10. **Your credit card processing fee could be higher.** Debit and credit card data are protected under the Payment Card Industry Data Security Standard (PCI DSS). You will be subject to higher transaction fees if your business is noncompliant. But that's not all—you could be fined up to $100,000 and have your relationship with your bank permanently terminated, which means you'll never be allowed to process credit cards again.

11. **The government will become involved.** If you have a cybersecurity breach, your company must report it to the Cybersecurity and Infrastructure Security Agency by emailing them at report@cisa.gov or calling 888-282-0870. Once you report it, CISA will coordinate with other federal agencies, such as the Federal Bureau of Investigation, to determine the severity of the breach. They may also provide you with guidance on how to prevent future breaches. While CISA will keep your report confidential, if the news does leak out, it could seriously damage your company's reputation. You must also report your breach to the applicable state authority.

12. **You might not find an MSP to take you on.** For an MSP, their reputation is everything. If one of their clients suffers irreparable damage from a cyberbreach, it can seriously stain their reputation. If your attitude is lackadaisical and you don't take compliance seriously as a culture, you might find it challenging to find an MSP willing to risk their reputation by taking you on as a client.

When it comes to compliance and cybersecurity, I often tell people they should think of their business the way they think about their house. You've got locks on all your doors and an alarm system. You can turn on all the alarms, but if someone leaves the back window open (someone clicks on a phishing email, the latest patches are not applied, etc.), it's easy for an intruder to walk right in and snoop around. I compare that to someone getting past your firewall.

Then, once they're in, hopefully your home will have sensors that will pick up the motion of someone who's not supposed to be there. That's similar to malware protection on your devices, which attempts to quarantine the invader and lock them down. However, if somebody evades the sensor, they will look for your valuables. They're going to search for where you keep your safe. The cybercriminal will search for your accounting-related passwords and where you keep your data.

If you choose not to protect yourself from these criminals, you're vulnerable to attacks daily and risk severe damage to your business.

Partnering with an MSP will substantially reduce your risk of being the target of a data breach, but you may still get hacked. While an MSP will do a comprehensive training program for your employees on identifying and avoiding clicking on phishing emails, we can't control the results. But here's the thing. If you do get breached, your MSP has put safeguards in place so the attacker won't be able to access your data and typically can get you back up and running again within a few hours.

If you don't have a recovery plan, the downtime could go on for weeks, even months, costing your business severely and perhaps even resulting in the permanent closing of your company. Plus, when you work with an MSP who can prove that you checked all the boxes and did everything right regarding compliance, you likely won't be the target of lawsuits or be asked to pay fines.

About Chad

Chad M. Brush is the founder and CEO of BE Connected, a technology management firm focusing on cybersecurity and compliance solutions in Nashville, Tennessee, and the surrounding area. He's also the founder and CEO of Brush Enterprises, an IT consulting company. Chad has been in IT since 1994, starting his career with Nashville-based Concepts In Communications. Chad worked his way up in various technology companies, becoming well-versed in the technology that companies need in order to thrive and protect themselves in today's rapidly changing business environment.

Chad founded BE Connected in 2017 because, throughout his years in the industry, he noticed that when a technology company would land a large enterprise company as a client, many of their smaller clients wouldn't get the attention they deserve. He was determined to change that. Chad is an advocate for companies that have been underserviced and oversold in the technology arena. When he told one of his clients how much his recommendations would save her business each month, she told him that dealing with him was "like winning the IT lottery."

The best part of Chad's job is that he gets to help people and ease their stress. He loves the relationships he has built with his clients, some of whom he initially met in the late 1990s and are now clients of BE Connected. That many of his clients have come from referrals is a tribute to the trust he's built up over the years with businesses in the Nashville area. A loyal and dependable professional, Chad consistently strives to improve himself and his BE Connected team daily.

Chad's drive to succeed was instilled in him at an early age. The firstborn son of a single mother, Chad was determined to help his mother put food on the table for him and his two older sisters and younger brother. Starting when he was eleven, Chad worked evenings and weekends, helping his mother succeed in her wallpapering business, one of three jobs she worked to make ends meet. This instilled in Chad a strong work ethic and a deep sense of loyalty and commitment. His detail-oriented attitude and trustworthiness make him an incredible asset to his clients and team.

Chad is very proud of the work BE Connected does with nonprofits such as Children Are People, which provides a safe, structured space where at-risk youth can learn, play, and flourish without their families being charged fees. Chad is passionate about working with and speaking to young entrepreneurial organizations about business IT, compliance, cybersecurity, and how to be an entrepreneur.

Chad and his wife, Kedran, live in Brentwood, Tennessee, with their dog, Bella. They are Tennessee Titans season ticket holders and big fans of the Nashville SC soccer club.

For more information, contact Chad at BE Connected:

Email: cbrush@beconnected.solutions
Phone: (615) 338-6720
Web: www.beconnected.solutions

Chapter 9

YOUR WORKFORCE IS YOUR BIGGEST CYBERSECURITY RISK; HERE'S EIGHT BEST PRACTICES YOU NEED TO MINIMIZE THE RISK

Paul Marchese

As a small or medium-sized business, you might spend a fortune on firewalls. You have the latest endpoint protection/antivirus apps. You use the best encryption software. You back up your data Every. Single. Day. Maybe you're doing everything YOU THINK you need to be doing as a company to minimize your cybersecurity risk, but in the blink of an eye, it can all be undone by a single employee's mistake.

In today's digital age, where cyberthreats are coming fast and furious, it's crucial to understand the role your employees play in keeping your organization secure. From lack of training and awareness to weak password practices and falling prey to phishing attacks, there are numerous ways your workforce can inadvertently expose your company to cyberthreats.

That's exactly what happened recently when an employee of the Consumer Financial Protection Bureau, an agency of the US government that protects consumers in the financial sector, committed a major breach by emailing the personal information of 256,000 consumers to a personal email account.[23]

To Err Is Human . . . And Cybercriminals Count On It

With all the warnings and information splashed across cyberspace to help employees be more secure online, how can scenes like the one I just mentioned keep playing out?

63

Well, it's simple. People think for themselves and make their own decisions—good or bad. Human error is inevitable. In fact, 95% of all security incidents and breaches are a result of human error.[24] The average hacker today stays on a machine/network for an average of 217 days. Why? It's simple. They want to gather all the data before they launch the attack to get a ransom from you!

The majority of cybersecurity breaches stem from human error rather than technical vulnerabilities. So, what are employees doing NOW that they need to stop doing YESTERDAY?

- **Falling for phishing attacks.** Employees frequently fall prey to email phishing attacks, unknowingly granting hackers access to sensitive information, whether it's through fake invoice scams, the new fake offer-based scams, unusual activity scams, or advance fee scams that come with a heartbreaking message from someone in another country begging for their help to recover a fortune (yep, people still fall for that one). More than 90% of successful cyberattacks begin with a phishing email.[25] Insufficient awareness and training in identifying phishing attacks leave employees wide open to threats.

- **Creating weak passwords.** Weak password practices pose a significant cybersecurity risk. Hackers can easily guess or crack weak passwords, especially when employees reuse them across multiple accounts. Failing to implement password complexity or regular password changes further exposes accounts to attack. Additionally, sharing passwords or writing them down puts sensitive information at risk.

- **Using unsecured networks.** Sure, the local coffeehouse might have big brand name recognition, but that doesn't mean the free Wi-Fi they offer is safe. When employees unknowingly connect to unsecured networks, it makes it easier for hackers to intercept sensitive information. Unsecured networks lack encryption, which makes your valuable data vulnerable to interception.

- **Misusing access privileges.** Employees with excessive access rights can unintentionally (or deliberately) compromise sensitive data, setting you up for a significant security risk. Unauthorized access, modifications, or theft can occur because of access privilege misuse, increasing the likelihood of insider threats and data breaches. I always recommend a regular look at what level of access is required for each of your employees to accomplish their job. They should never have greater access than is required.

- **Bringing your own devices.** Okay, since BYOD and remote work go hand in hand these days, it's not so simple to completely cut them out. Because most people already have their own smartphone and laptop, some businesses are opting to let employees use them to do their jobs. Sure, it might save you on hardware costs, but the havoc wreaked by hacking, malware, and data leakage isn't cheap if devices aren't protected!

Computing mistakes made by employees can be extremely COSTLY in more ways than one. First, there's the loss or theft of sensitive data. Second, there is the financial loss, including legal and regulatory fines, remediation costs, and lost productivity. Third, there's the damage to your company's reputation and the erosion of your customers' trust.

Don't panic—all hope is not lost. You CAN turn your employees into human firewalls. You might ask, what is a human firewall? It's an employee who 1) thinks before clicking, 2) knows what should be going on and when it isn't, 3) respects and follows security policies, and 4) says something when they see something! Employees can be your first line of defense instead of your weakest link in preventing cybersecurity events.

To help you minimize the role of human error in your cybersecurity strategy, I've put together eight best practices that my own clients have found success with.

1. Make Regular Cybersecurity Awareness Training Mandatory

This practice wasn't just randomly placed in the #1 position. It is the NUMBER ONE way you can help minimize the security risks that your employees pose. And the important word here to remember is "regular." Ongoing employee training and education play a crucial role in increasing awareness of phishing, vulnerabilities, and other cybersecurity risks.

But *how* you train is just as important. If you want it to "stick," you've got to make it impactful. The first rule: It has to be mandatory. No free passes for anyone, even the owners!

To keep training relevant and interesting, incorporate a variety of printed and online materials, including posters, infographics, and newsletters. Provide simulated phishing exercises to help employees identify different types of phishing and social engineering attacks. Always encourage employees—when in doubt, they should avoid clicking on suspicious links and instead seek advice.

And DO give them tests after each training session. This is a good way to help you find the weakest links who may need additional training. The training we recommend gives the management team a breakdown of every person so you can see who needs some extra help. There will always be at least one employee who is more likely to fall for a scam or click on a phishing link. It's next to impossible to weed out all high-risk employees—remember, to err is human, so just make sure those employees are always learning and always making progress.

2. Implement Strong Password Policies

Password fatigue, anyone? We've all experienced it. That crushing feeling of anxiety and mental exhaustion from trying to remember and keep track of a gazillion passwords both at home and at work. But it's a necessary evil if you want to guard against cyber-attacks. Here's why: 81% of company data breaches were caused by poor passwords, and 80% of hacking incidents were caused by stolen and reused login information.[26]

Implementing strong password policies is crucial to protecting sensitive information and preventing unauthorized access. Businesses need to require that their employees use long and complex passwords with at least fourteen characters, including capital and lowercase letters, numbers, and special characters. They also should be changing passwords on a regular basis—at least two times per year. In conjunction, implement multifactor authentication to add an extra layer of protection. Additionally, enforcing password encryption and storage protocols further strengthens the overall security posture. You can get a password manager for your company as well. This stores the passwords in a fully encrypted format and protects them against a hacker gaining access. DO NOT EVER keep your password in a Word document or Excel spreadsheet that is unencrypted. The file minimally needs to be password-protected, and remember that your PC remembers passwords as well, making it easy for you to log in to your sites but making it equally easy for hackers to gain the same access.

3. Update/Patch Software Often

Believe it or not, even though they're reminded often, many employees still don't bother to update their software when there is a new patch. And if your employees are using their own devices for work—forget it! The reason is basically that they just don't understand how important these software updates are.

Outdated software can contain vulnerabilities that can be exploited by cyber-criminals. Businesses should adopt a proactive approach to software management, ensuring that all systems and applications are regularly updated with the latest security patches. This simple yet effective practice reduces the risk of cyberattacks and data breaches. If your employee is using a BYOD machine, then you should protect yourself from exposure as well by requiring a minimum set of security standards and protections.

4. Require VPN Usage When Employees Are Out of the Office

If a Wi-Fi network doesn't require employees to enter a password or login credentials—they shouldn't be using it! These open networks have unencrypted connections, and hackers, cybersnoops, and other bad actors are just waiting to steal their login passwords, credit card info, communications, and other personal data.

VPNs or secure remote control of a machine will keep your company's data safe inside the network, which makes working from home safer for your employees by protecting their online activities from bad actors.

Make sure the dangers of connecting to unsecured networks are part of your cyber awareness training program, and make VPNs a part of your Internet policies and procedures.

5. Implement Proper Access Management

While not as prevalent a security risk, insider breaches do occasionally happen. It could be an angry employee, a third-party vendor, or a contractor who might decide to maliciously access your customers' sensitive data. Balancing security with efficiency can be a challenge for businesses. You want to make sure employees have the minimum set of access rights to do their job—but nothing more! The more privileges and access employees have, the greater the potential for risk. Hackers salivate over privileged accounts and credentials because they can gain access to your company's everything!

That's why you need to implement strict access controls and provide regular audits to help mitigate the risk of access misuse. Proper access management helps prevent unauthorized access by limiting unnecessary access rights. By implementing these measures, you can reduce the chances of data breaches and protect your organization from potential security incidents.

If you do rely on third-party vendors, make sure you can access and monitor their security practices. A vendor risk-management program can help you identify potential vulnerabilities and ensure that vendors adhere to your cybersecurity standards.

6. Use Automation to Monitor Systems

Remember this: Humans make mistakes. And as much as you do to help minimize the chances that one of your employees will compromise your cybersecurity, things will happen. That's where automation comes in. Automation can help reduce human error with quicker and more efficient detection and response to security threats.

Additionally, automation helps enforce consistent security policies throughout the organization and continuously scans for vulnerabilities and potential breaches. Partnering with a managed IT services provider that uses the latest technology and automated monitoring and cybersecurity protection systems can be a beneficial part of your company's cybersecurity strategy.

MSPs offer specialized expertise and resources that help bolster cybersecurity defenses, including real-time monitoring and alerts, enabling proactive threat management and machine lockdown so you can prevent unauthorized access. Moreover, automation can streamline the patching and updating process, minimizing vulnerabilities. Most of the time, this automation is done overnight so as not to interrupt normal business productivity.

7. Improve BYOD Security Risks

Since BYOD work environments are here to stay, your company should implement some strict guidelines and practices that can help improve security risks specific to a personal smartphone, laptop, and tablet used for work. For example, even if employees are using them on their secured Wi-Fi connections, they should still use a VPN when accessing company data. Also, install mobile device management software so data can be remotely wiped should the device become lost or stolen. Additionally, BYODs should be scanned on a regular basis for malware and other security threats. Remember, these devices are accessing your company data, so requiring a minimum set of security standards is not out of the norm.

8. Create a Security-Focused Culture

When you make cybersecurity a part of your company's DNA, it becomes something bigger than what happens in a training class, and it goes a long way toward minimizing human error. Security is considered with every daily decision your employees—including C-level leaders—make. In a security-focused culture, open dialogue and questions are encouraged, education is continuous, and proactive security behavior is rewarded.

Conclusion

We've seen it time and again with high-profile cyberattack cases where human error is a significant contributor. Without proper training and awareness, your employees can unknowingly put your organization at risk. From falling victim to phishing attacks to weak password practices, each employee needs to understand their role in maintaining a secure environment. Encouraging them to take ownership of their role in safeguarding sensitive information helps create a security-conscious culture.

Remember, cybersecurity is a collective responsibility, and by investing in your workforce's cybersecurity knowledge and skills, you are investing in the overall security and success of your business. You are not "too small" to be hacked, as hackers don't really care how big you are. It's not *if*, it's *when* you will be hacked and how much you are prepared to pay to recover your data from the hackers. Now go create those human firewalls so you can start building that extra layer of protection!

About Paul

Paul Marchese is the president and owner of Marchese Computer Products, Inc. Founded in 1981, MCP is the oldest technology consultant and managed services provider in Western New York.

Marchese Computer Products specializes in security and technology solutions for small and medium-sized businesses in the Western and Central New York areas.

Paul's expertise in IT began when he founded MCP even before he finished his college career. He specialized in information technology and telecommunications and spent much of his time helping companies use technology as a tool to move their businesses forward. In 1997, he designed and developed the only data- and web-hosting facility in Genesee, Livingston, Orleans, and Wyoming Counties of Western New York.

Today, Paul has built Marchese Computer Products into one of WNY's most responsive and reliable managed services providers, serving more than two hundred small and medium-sized businesses that use technology to maximize their growth and opportunities. His technical team of eight has extensive industry expertise in a wide range of services and skills, including workstations, servers, networks, phone systems, video systems, software, and printers.

Paul holds a Bachelor of Arts in computer science and mathematics from the University of Rochester and has more than forty years of experience in information technology.

He is the author of *Business Owner's Guide To Cyber Security*, published in October 2020, a guide with tips and strategies on maximizing technology to create better business outcomes. He followed up in early 2022 with *Social Media Cyber Attacks: The New Frontier*, detailing how hackers are using social media to gain access.

Paul was chosen as a featured presenter of the first annual Small Business Tech Day in 2022 in Buffalo, New York, alongside celebrity presenters like *Shark Tank's* Kevin O'Leary, former FBI counterterrorism and counterintelligence operative Eric O'Neill, and bestselling author and entrepreneur Mike Michalowicz. When Paul isn't working, he volunteers his time as a member of the board of directors for the Genesee County YMCA (GLOW YMCA) and as the IT administrator for Rotary District 7090.

For more information, contact Paul at Marchese Computer Products:

Email: paul@mcpinc.com
Phone: (585) 343-2713
Web: www.mcpinc.com
LinkedIn: www.linkedin.com/in/paul-marchese-mcp/
Address: 220 Ellicott Street, Batavia, NY 14020

Chapter 10

WHY EMPLOYEE EDUCATION IS YOUR FIRST LINE OF DEFENSE

Zac Abdulkadir

Not too long ago, an employee at a large construction company logged in to their email. He scrolled through unread inbox messages, accepted meeting invitations, and reviewed tracking details for an Amazon or UPS delivery. These fifteen minutes of email scrolling sound like what I do every day; it's perhaps what you see in your inbox too. But a few hours later, the employee noticed emails had been sent to company customers from his email address. He wasn't doing it, so who was? The employee realized the issue—his email had been hacked.

When the CEO heard the news from the company's internal IT team, he said, "Don't we spend $10,000 a month on a software package to prevent issues like this? Call *them* and find out why it happened!"

This is an actual situation that a client of ours found themselves in a few months ago. My company, Netready, supports their internal IT team. The CEO was right to be mad. The situation was avoidable, but it wasn't the software's fault. At some point, this employee fell for a phishing attempt—a popular technique where a cybercriminal poses as a legitimate person or business to steal information. Behind malware, it's the second most common cyberattack on small businesses.[27] It's also the most financially damaging, costing breached organizations an average of $4.91 million every year.

Security software stops many spam emails like phishing scams from getting into your inboxes, but it's not the be-all and end-all of your security infrastructure. Cyber-criminals use techniques like social engineering (psychological manipulation) to get people to give away confidential information. That's why the core problem in this event wasn't the software—it was the employee.

Employees are your weakest link. They are also your first line of defense. It's your job to ensure they have the resources to be a formidable frontline against the never-ending barrage of cyberattacks.

Technology Can't Be Your Savior

If the construction company had been breached twenty years ago, the CEO probably would've been right about blame lying within a system vulnerability. Until the mid-2000s, breaches were primarily technical. Hackers wrote custom codes to bypass firewalls or scanned the Internet for vulnerable servers to access confidential information.

However, as technology improved over time, it became much harder to bypass advanced systems. In the mid-2000s, cybercriminals adapted their tactics and started targeting a vulnerability with much weaker defenses—people.[28] They figured out that it's a lot easier to get inside companies via their employees who use the same simple passwords over again and have no idea what a phishing scam is. All hackers need to do is ask, and many people will hand over all kinds of personal information.

All Hackers Have to Do Is Ask

During an episode of *Jimmy Kimmel Live*, a segment was aired called "What Is Your Password?" An interviewer asked passersby a series of innocent questions with a covert mission: to get them to give away their passwords on camera.[29] In a shockingly short amount of time, people gave away pet names, birth dates, and graduation years—admitting those are the same words they reuse in personal passwords. If these interviews hadn't been recorded live, it would be almost unbelievable. People will, quite literally, give away their passwords. All you have to do is ask.

Hackers won't admit who they are; instead, they'll use a few simple tactics to manipulate unsuspecting victims into believing they are someone else (and thus perfectly safe to share information with). In a 2015 documentary called *Real Future*, a volunteer lets hacker Jess attempt to breach his cell phone account at the DEF CON hacker conference in Las Vegas, one of the world's largest annual hacker conventions.[30] My team goes every year to keep up with the latest trends in hacking, and the convention is so risky that you can't bring your credit card or cell phone in. Well, you can, but you'll get hacked. In the video, Jess uses "vishing" (voice solicitation) with no tools other than a recording of a crying baby and a cell phone to hack the volunteer's personal cell phone account.

Within a few minutes, she successfully contacted the volunteer's cell provider, got his email address, added herself to his account, changed his password, and locked him out of his account completely—right in front of him. Luckily, this was just for show, and Jess happily gave the volunteer the information he needed to regain access to his account.

But this kind of hack happens every day to real people, particularly in small businesses. In fact, small businesses experience 350% more social engineering attacks than larger companies.[31]

Hackers bypass traditional technical defenses and gain unauthorized access to data by exploiting human trust, curiosity, and lack of awareness. Emails, QR codes, public Wi-Fi, Jimmy Kimmel interviews—cybercriminals are using every tactic available and banking on us making a mistake. Which we do. Often.

Yes, Your Young, Hip Employees Will Fall For It Too

CEOs often tell me, "My employees are young, they're hip, they don't fall for this kind of stuff." *Anybody* can fall for this kind of stuff. These are professional criminals who use the latest technology and knowledge of modern human behavior to get us to do precisely what we shouldn't. It has nothing to do with whether your workforce is old, young, or tech-savvy. If you catch somebody on the right day, like when they're expecting an Amazon or UPS package, the hacker *will* get lucky.

You'd be surprised what people give away their passwords for. I've had CEOs click on phony password-reset emails for Microsoft accounts (Microsoft is the #1 most impersonated company by phishers[32]), and employees fall for gift card scams, spending hundreds of dollars of their own money. Anybody can fall for a well-crafted email, and with AI and ChatGPT widely available, looking for grammatical errors or misspellings won't always help you spot an email written by a criminal.

If you don't train your employees on what to do and what to look out for, they will fall victim to an attack. Employee education and security awareness training must be your first defense to keep hackers out and your data in.

Security Awareness Training Works

One of my clients is a private aviation company that charters jets for wealthy families and big corporate companies. A few months ago, they worked with a vendor to organize a month-long trip to Europe for a client. They went back and forth on questions about catering and other requests. Then the customer service agent at the aviation company received an email from the vendor. It read, "Hey, we transferred money from the wrong account. Could you refund it to us? Then we'll transfer the money back to you from a different account." The agent thought the email sounded weird, so she returned to the previous emails and made a critical observation. The vendor email was one letter off. Instead of so-and-so@premierjets, it said so-and-so@premierijets. Did you catch the difference?

There's an extra "i" in the second email. It turned out that the vendor they were working with had been breached. Hackers were in their email system searching for people who transferred money to them in the past, including our client.

As our client, the aviation company employees had been participating in security awareness training for two years. Once a month, we'd send a three- to five-minute video on a relevant topic. After the video, employees answered a few questions. The company avoided a terrible situation because the employee knew what red flags to look for. They contacted us, and we alerted the vendor. Within a day or two, the vendor admitted they had a breach and were working to secure it.

Others don't make out so well, especially those who don't take advantage of employee education. I've seen SMBs pay $750,000 to get their data back (plus months of recovery and whatever ransom they paid to have the data returned). I've seen business owners close their doors—and end their twenty-year careers—after a preventable ransomware attack. It's devastating to get that call too late. But stopping this kind of thing from happening keeps me going in this industry because I know it doesn't have to happen. Educating yourself and your employees is the first and most critical step in protecting your business.

Our cyber-awareness training costs $30 a user per year and takes less than six minutes a month to complete. We know that if employees receive consistent, practical security awareness training and use it, this reduces an organization's risk of a socially engineered attack by up to 70%.[33] It's a no-brainer. But not all employee education is created equal.

Great Employee Education = Security + Productivity

Your employees want to be productive so they can go home to their families, take their dogs for a walk, or have a drink with their friends after work. We all have things we want to do when our workday ends, which sometimes causes us to rush through our emails and not pay attention like we should. When security is layered on thick, like strong email filters, hours-long training, or a computer screen that automatically locks up after fifteen seconds, it slows our work down, so we avoid security behaviors in favor of productivity.

What I hear the most from clients regarding security awareness training is that they want to balance productivity and security. Our job as security professionals is to determine what tools we can put in place and what kind of education we can provide employees to make security easy *and* accessible for an organization without impeding productivity.

Many business leaders who realize they must have employee education to comply with HIPAA, PCI, or their cyber insurance company will say to me, "Okay, we'll order pizza and host an annual training. It's just once a year, right? Security plus productivity. Right?"

Wrong.

By the time an annual training comes out, the cybergame has changed. The key is balance. Harp on security too much, and employees will get fatigued and possibly tune it out. Talk about it too little, and cybercriminals' tactics will have changed so much that the content is out of date. What *does* work is consistent, bite-sized training that reflects the most common and relevant threats to employees.

Once a month, we send employees an email that introduces a security topic. They're asked to watch a three- to four-minute video and answer a few basic questions. In less than six minutes, they're back to work. Short, frequent videos provide critical education about common threats and how to stop them and increase employees' confidence in their ability to detect and prevent hacks.

Our videos cover topics like:

- Where NOT to enter your password
- What voicemail phishing is
- How to identify email red flags
- Dangers of public Wi-Fi and USB ports

Another part of security awareness training we do with clients is phishing tests. Every month, each user is sent a test phishing email to see if they fall for it or not. It takes no additional time out of their day. We review the results with an HR manager or office manager every quarter for about fifteen minutes.

None of this training stops employees from writing their reports, making calls, or doing whatever they need to get done. Five to six minutes of your day once a month is all it takes to reduce by a large margin your organization's risk of attack.

Defend Your Company from Within

Security demands a multilayered approach; every layer needs to be as strong as the next. Your first and most formidable line of defense is your employees because that's where hackers will attack first. Your employee cybersecurity awareness training must be as robust as your technical and physical security. Many companies forget that, and it costs them dearly.

Our organization makes security training part of everything we do without compromising productivity, and we help our clients do the same. Ultimately, it's up to you to implement and enforce employee education in your company and ensure they have the tools and support they need to be productive *and* secure every day. Because you must be right all the time; hackers only need to be lucky once.

About Zac

Zac Abdulkadir realized the critical role of cybersecurity in business earlier than most managed services providers in the IT industry. Zac founded his Los Angeles-based cybersecurity firm, Netready, in 1995. By 2009, Zac was considered a trusted cybersecurity expert in the field by many companies across dozens of industries while many IT companies were still operating as break-fixes. During this time, Zac often explored security boundaries through hobby hacking. When he revealed an exploit in the major Internet services provider EarthLink, he became concerned. If he could expose a critical system vulnerability with relative ease, so could hackers with more malicious motivations. Zac knew small and midsized businesses were unprepared for what was coming and made it his mission to ensure they were protected.

As technology advanced over the following decade, so did the prevalence of cyberattacks and the need for businesses to implement robust security measures to defend against cyberthreats. Zac remembers receiving a call from a CPA too late: Without the necessary protections, his firm was breached. There was nothing he could do, and Zac was devastated as he watched the business owner close the doors of his CPA firm after two successful decades of operation. Zac believes catastrophic loss like this doesn't have to happen, and he's committed himself and the skilled Netready team to safeguard organizations from preventable cyber risks.

Today, as CEO and chief information security officer of Netready, Zac relentlessly pursues the most effective and innovative strategies, using cutting-edge technologies in the field. Zac's team has earned some of the highest certifications in the industry, including CISSP, CISA, CISM, CRISC, MCSE, CCNA, VCP, and ITIL.

While robust technology is essential in an effective security framework, Zac firmly believes that employees are the first line of defense in any company's security. He champions the concept that practical employee awareness training is the cornerstone of effective cybersecurity. Drawing on his extensive expertise, Zac educates his clients on the importance of user training and dismisses the misconception that it needs to be overly complex. Instead, he highlights the power of short, relevant videos that teach employees how to identify and mitigate the most common cyberthreats. By instilling this culture of alertness and education, organizations can significantly reduce the risk of costly cyber incidents and prevent disastrous attacks.

As an accomplished cybersecurity professional with over twenty-five years of experience, Zac leverages his expertise to design innovative solutions for all Netready clients. The cybersecurity firm's holistic approach encompasses technical defenses, as well as comprehensive training and education programs, to empower employees as the first line of defense. By combining his extensive industry knowledge, real-world insights, and passionate drive to protect businesses, Zac is dedicated to helping organizations fortify their security and prevent cyber incidents before they ever happen.

For more information, contact Zac at Netready:

Email: Zac@NetreadyIT.com
Phone: (714) 986-5701
Web: www.NetreadyIT.com
LinkedIn: www.linkedin.com/in/zac-abdulkadir/

Chapter 11

HOW TO INSPIRE ENTHUSIASTIC CYBERSECURITY COMPLIANCE FROM EVERY EMPLOYEE

Robin Cole

Rule followers and rule breakers—every organization has them. Each one of your employees falls somewhere along a spectrum of rule adherence. If you're lucky, maybe most of your employees are inclined to follow the rules. They take their leftovers out of the fridge at the end of the day, join team meetings on time, and consistently meet work deadlines. When most employees do these things, your business machine operates smoothly. However, when it comes to cybersecurity compliance, you are only as strong as your most security-apathetic employee (even if 99% of your employees follow compliance rules). The World Economic Forum reports that 95% of all cybersecurity breaches are related to human error.[34] So, whether you have one black sheep or five, they are your organization's weakest link, and getting them to follow the rules is a challenging task—a critical one.

The explosion of work from home has exacerbated the problem by drastically increasing the attack surface. Like a glass of water, we began passing around our work computers to other family members, thus increasing our exposure to all kinds of risk we'd never be exposed to in an office setting. In the two years following the beginning of the COVID-19 pandemic, cyberattacks on small businesses rose by 150%.[35] Many poor security practices continue in companies today, whether we return to our offices or work from home. All it takes is a single click on a harmful email link to damage your reputation, shut your business down for days, and cost you thousands of dollars in ransoms, fines, or lost business.

> *"The biggest cybersecurity threats are inside your company."*
> —Harvard Business Review

Getting your employees to adhere to compliance rules is crucial to running a successful modern business. In fact, it's required by most regulators today. But if you've done the annual training, purchased password managers, and tried simulated phishing tests and you continue to see Post-it notes stuck to computer monitors or have employees clicking on simulated phishing emails, you're not alone. Many business leaders struggle to consistently convince their employees to comply with their organization's cybersecurity controls reliably. Why do employees resist security training? Why do they forget simple rules? And how do you get them to abide enthusiastically with cybersecurity compliance—something so important to your business?

While no method of garnering security compliance from your employees is 100% effective, a new approach to security training is entering the cybersecurity industry with great success—gamification. It leverages human psychology to encourage enthusiastic participation in compliance and helps you cultivate an entire culture around cybersecurity that will significantly lower your risk of attacks, save you money, and protect the future of your business.

Why Employees Resist Traditional Security Awareness Training

There are two primary reasons employees don't participate in compliance effectively: 1) it's not relatable to their lives, and 2) it's not interesting.

1. Employees Don't Believe Compliance Is Important Until It's Too Late

In 2018, the Hawaii Emergency Management Agency (HI-EMA) sent out a warning to the public that said, "BALLISTIC MISSILE THREAT INBOUND TO HAWAII. SEEK IMMEDIATE SHELTER. THIS IS NOT A DRILL." But it was a mistake. The announcement was supposed to air as a test, but a "problem employee" pushed the wrong button. The event flooded news channels, and the organization came under severe scrutiny. Soon, a photo published a few months prior of an operations officer in the organization's headquarters revealed a visible sticky note with a password on a computer in the background.[36] They claimed the password was expired and a breach was not a cause of the false alarm. However, the organization was ultimately found to have some serious security missteps.

Too often, employees don't change their behavior until *after* an attack like this. By then, it's too late. Multiple HI-EMA employees resigned after the incident, which could have been avoided with appropriate compliance behaviors.

Humans tend not to care about consequences that aren't directly related to their own lives. Twenty-seven percent of US employees of large companies said they would sell their credentials to criminals, according to a SailPoint survey.[37] If employees don't believe in the value of cybersecurity compliance, they won't do it. If a computer is set to time out after a period of not being used, a fifteen-character password must be typed in, and two-factor authentication entered time and again takes time away from productive work. Looking for shortcuts, we write the ones we use most on sticky notes placed handily and exposed on our desks.

2. Typical Security Training Is Snooze-Worthy and Ineffective

Humans aren't born with an intrinsic understanding of the value of cybersecurity. We must be taught. The problem is that traditional cybersecurity training—a four-hour annual training—is monotonous and ineffective. Employees don't remember tedious annual daylong sessions. Additionally, they aren't up-to-date with the latest cyberattack trends, so trends have likely changed even if they recall the information.

Segmented processes for security training programs are also admired in cybersecurity training circles. Organizations provide training that combines simulated phishing attacks—and when employees fail, they send them to a brief training session. Those who keep getting sent *to the gulag* may be criticized for having a "propensity to click" and take risks. People who are *not* falling for the attacks are not sent away for training or subject to criticism.

Lackluster training methods don't help employees understand *why* the training is important to *them*. However, if business leaders leverage human psychology in a positive way, they can stimulate cooperation with a key to enthusiastic cybersecurity engagement. The key: Gamification.

What Is Gamification?

"Gamification is 75% psychology and 25% technology," says Gabe Zichermann, coauthor of the book *Gamification By Design*. There are many ways you can boost cybersecurity training so that it's not terrible. You can try sending short weekly videos and quizzes and offer incentives for good behavior, like a free lunch or gift cards to favorite coffee shops. But research shows our brains are 68% more engaged in training when we enjoy it.[38]

The term "gamification" was coined in 2002 by Nick Pelling and can be defined as "the application of gaming mechanics to non-gaming contexts with the aim of inducing engagement and raising levels of motivation."[39] Since the mid-2000s, gamification has been used in navigation apps like Waze, educational apps like Duolingo, and fitness programs like Nike Run Club. Increasingly, companies are bringing gamification into the workplace. It combines the things that make games fun—storylines, relatable characters, points, badges, leveling, and competition—with training content to excite *and* educate employees to learn, engage, and have some fun while they're at it.

In 2014, Cisco gamified its Social Media Training Program using team challenges and the incentives of certifications so different levels of employees could learn about social media related to their roles in the organization.[40] Similarly, when Deloitte gamified its Deloitte Leadership Academy using missions, badges, and leaderboards, they had a 37% increase in users every week.[41] Salesforce's free learning platform, Trailhead, awards users with badges, points, and an internal recognition program as they make their way through modules and courses. Between 2019 and 2021, they saw a 180% increase in badge completions.

Gamification in Cybersecurity

In cybersecurity awareness training, you teach your employees safe behaviors and help them understand that negative consequences occur when they don't consistently employ safe behaviors. Some organizations have adopted gamification in their cybersecurity awareness training to make security concepts more relatable and, dare I say it—fun!

Deloitte designed an office escape room where five to six participants must solve seven challenges in twenty minutes to complete the game.[42] For example, to complete the challenge, the group goes through some or all of the following activities:

- Secure a laptop infected with ransomware to protect and preserve critical evidence needed for forensic analysis.
- Identify social engineering intrusions, phishing emails, or vishing attacks (voicemail and text messages) to prevent threat actors from gaining access to organization data.

- Recognize password vulnerabilities and create a strong password and multi-factor authentication to keep hackers out of accounts.
- Spot breaches and take the proper steps to isolate the breach (disconnect the computer from the Internet, but don't shut it off) and notify the right individuals that a breach is underway.

Terranova Security similarly designed their Serious Game.[43] In this immersive virtual game, employees participate in ten-minute modules to complete mini-tasks, answer skill-based questions, and try out their security skills in real-world simulations. Terranova implements an out-of-the-box training approach that addresses key psychological factors, stating, "By allowing players to solve virtual puzzles and interact with immersive narratives, you're tapping into innate human psychology to ensure your training is always engaging, informative, and fun for all participants."

Infosec offers a free interactive demo of their Choose Your Own Adventure Security Awareness Games[44] where you can experience gamified space-themed training for yourself. Playing the space engineer role, you decide how to complete your mission. Done correctly, you prevent villainous infiltration, successfully repair the ship's hull, and protect data for every being in the solar system—oh, and learn essential facts about social engineering and compliance rules in the process!

Benefits of Gamification in Cybersecurity Awareness Training

Gamification is designed to work with human psychology, not against it. By understanding what motivates employees, training becomes fun and results in lasting benefits to an organization's culture of cybersecurity.

Changes Behaviors

Gamified cybersecurity awareness training is risk-free and relatable. Security escape rooms or immersive simulated training modules give employees the experience of a cyber incident without the consequences. For example, in Infosec's demo, users must decide whether to let visitors onto the ship. One visitor sends a link for the user to verify their credentials. Unexpected links appear in our emails daily, making the training highly relevant and applicable. When training is done this way, employees understand the impact *before* an attack, not after, and are more likely to exhibit security-positive behaviors.[45]

Increases Participation

Gamification techniques are interactive. Whether your gamified training is an escape room, video game, or virtual mystery-style challenge, employees enjoy an immersive experience that includes clues, characters, storylines, scoreboards, and incentives. They keep coming back to obtain higher scores, compete with colleagues, or just have fun.[46]

Encourages Intrinsic Motivation

Scoreboards and point systems leverage intrinsic motivations by challenging users to better their best, whether working to beat their last score or participating in an internal, friendly competition amongst co-workers.[47] If your training hosts team challenges, that can also foster a sense of belonging and meaning in the training that's hard to promote in other training approaches.

Increases Confidence

The more employees practice their security skills by completing missions, earning badges, or beating a level, the more confidently they can handle real-world challenges.

Improves Retention

Research shows that storytelling unlocks our attention span.[48] Relatable characters, entertaining storylines, and challenges that appear in gamified training are relatable and exciting to us; thus, they become better encoded in our minds. Additionally, experiential learning boosts retention after two weeks by more than 68% compared to studying a concept, according to EdgePoint Learning.[49]

Supports an Organization-Wide Culture of Cybersecurity

When your employees have fun completing their cybersecurity training, it contributes to a robust organization-wide culture of cybersecurity that's necessary to protect your organization in a landscape riddled with threat actors sending attacks your team's way every single day. It reinforces good behavior without punishing unsafe behavior, encouraging a crucial team mentality in cybersecurity—"See something, say something." When employees fear retaliation for bad behavior, they'll protect themselves and their colleagues by staying silent when a mistake puts the organization at risk.

Imagine if astronaut Jack Swigert—because he feared backlash or consequences for himself or team members—never reported, "Ah, Houston, we've had a problem here," as unexpected warning lights were triggered in Apollo 13? The spacecraft—and those inside—may never have returned home safely. If your organization's culture is rooted in positive reinforcement, your team will feel more comfortable reporting, "Houston, we have a problem," when an unexpected breach shows up. Together, you can quickly guide your organization away from devastating consequences.

Saves Money on Cyber Insurance

If you show your insurance company you have a well-honed, well-maintained, and enthusiastic culture of cybersecurity, it'll save you money and hassle too. Insurance policies include a list of over 150 questions, and that list is growing. When they ask, "Do you want to add anything?" you'll say, "Yes!" and demonstrate how you reinforce the security culture through gamified training programs. You'll stand out as a low-risk organization, so they may charge you less than companies ignoring risks.

Makes Employees Happier

A 2019 study by TalentLMS found that 88% of employees said gamification makes them feel happier during training,[50] and 33% said they want more gamification elements in workplace training. Happy employees, happy life. Isn't that what they say?

Level Up Your Cybersecurity Compliance

There are a million reasons to be annoyed with cybersecurity compliance. It takes time and money to implement the processes necessary to be compliant. But all your work to be compliant can be out the window at a moment's notice if your employees don't comply. The trick to enthusiastic compliance—to turn rule breakers into rule followers—is to encourage participation by gamifying your security awareness training.

People need to *believe* that security is essential, and they need to have fun. When they do, they become proactive protectors of your organization's most vital digital assets instead of the internal threat that gives them away. Try gamifying your cybersecurity awareness training, and let me know how it goes for your organization. I'll see you on the leaderboards!

About Robin

Ham radio and a high school science project (where he designed and built an analog computer) sparked T. Robin Cole III's early interest in math and science. Those experiences led him to his Bachelor of Science in electrical engineering. During his college years, as Robin's initial fascination with digital computing first gained traction, he also embarked on another lifelong passion—flying. As a general aviation pilot, Robin is exhilarated each time he sheds the surly bonds of Earth.

Upon completing his undergraduate studies, Robin ventured from the Midwest to New York City, where he enrolled at New York University, seeking to extend his expertise beyond engineering into corporate finance. At first, he worked as a systems engineer on cutting-edge military aviation electronics until an inviting opportunity appeared for him to pivot onto Wall Street. Leveraging his education, Robin spent two decades working in high levels of the bond market, advising large institutional investors. Years of observing how large businesses identify, evaluate, finance, and adopt innovative technologies to enhance their competitive strengths prepared him to help small and medium businesses do the same.

During his early years of professional growth, Robin also married, raised two wonderful children, and joined two school boards, acting on his belief in education and community engagement. In 2003, Robin was drawn back to his family's business, the Rite Group, which has operated in the Southeast Missouri region since 1967. As president of the Rite Group, Robin reignited his love for digital technology. He dedicates his knowledge and experience to helping small and medium businesses leverage digital technologies that advance and strengthen their competitive advantages.

Robin feels grateful for the many fulfilling opportunities he enjoys, and he devotes time to volunteer service with nonprofit organizations, including Cape Area Habitat for Humanity, Cape Girardeau Public Schools Foundation, Cape Girardeau Airport Advisory Board, AOPA's Airport Support Network, United Way of Southeast Missouri, Cape Girardeau Career & Technology Center, Southeast Missouri State University/Donald L. Harrison College of Business and Computing, and the Rotary Club of Cape Girardeau.

In 2015, the Federal Aviation Administration distinguished Robin with its prestigious Wright Brothers Master Pilot Award. When Robin is not dancing the skies on laughter-silvered wings or spending time with his children and grandson, he satisfies an insatiable thirst for knowledge, seeking new avenues for exploration. Robin eagerly anticipates the future and the endless possibilities that technology and personal growth will bring, fully embracing the best days of his life.

For more information, contact Robin at the Rite Group:

Email: trcole3@theritegroup.com
Phone: (573) 369-9345
Web: www.theritegroup.com
LinkedIn: www.linkedin.com/in/trobincole/

Chapter 12

WHY COMPLIANCE AS A CULTURE MUST BE TAKEN SERIOUSLY FROM THE TOP DOWN

Gregory Mauer

When Joe was a kid, his dad had a Corvette. Bright red and sleek, a shimmering flash of metal as it raced by at ninety-eight miles per hour. Joe's dad liked to drive fast. *Really* fast. He didn't go fast only on country backroads; he drove fast everywhere. Still, he looked out for cop cars, and Joe even remembers his father installing a radar detector to alert him of nearby police cars. Joe's dad did all of this because he loved to go *fast*. Speed was exhilarating—it made him feel alive. Nevertheless, Joe's dad was breaking a very simple regulation. Three words on a white sign: "Speed Limit 65."

Soon, Joe grew up and passed his own driver's test. He saved some money, and I'm sure you can guess what he did with it. Joe bought a fast car. It was a solid black Mustang with two thick white racing stripes the length of the car. Like his dad, Joe took every opportunity to careen his pride and joy down country roads and zip through highway traffic. He never got a ticket, so he kept doing it. The more he sped without consequences, the more risks he took. When Joe got in his car, he didn't even look at the speedometer. Eventually, he got pulled over. But a $100 ticket here and there wasn't a big deal. In his mind, it was such a small amount to pay; he'd rather fork over the cash than waste his life driving slowly.

But one night, Joe sped down the highway, clocking around 110 mph. It was late, and Joe had most of the dark stretch of road to himself. Suddenly, he faced a blinding flash of white lights. A drunk driver had crossed the median into Joe's lane. They collided head-on.

Thankfully, Joe survived the crash and was hospitalized only for minor injuries. The other driver wasn't as lucky; he was pronounced dead on the scene. Later, a police investigator told Joe that the other driver had been drunk, which is what caused him to cross the median into Joe's lane. Joe considered himself a victim, but others weren't so convinced of his innocence. After police investigated the scene, measuring tire tracks, reviewing drug tests, and pulling driving records, Joe's track record of speeding was revealed. The drunk driver's family hired an attorney, who argued that Joe was partly to blame for the accident.

The rule is simple: Speed Limit 65. But Joe repeatedly broke the law, and now he faced severe consequences. Fines, investigations, thousands of dollars of medical bills, attorney fees, and a lawsuit from the other driver's family threatened to take every penny Joe had.

Freedom of Choice, Not Freedom from Consequences

I don't know Joe. This isn't a story that happened to me or someone I know. But Joe's story is important because we can imagine how he ended up in this situation. He repeatedly broke a simple law and eventually paid the price.

But, for some reason, compliance isn't as easy for business leaders to understand. I know many CEOs playing the same game as Joe and his father—disregarding simple compliance and regulation rules to keep running their business as they've always done. While you have the freedom of choice, like Joe, you don't have freedom from consequences.

You Call the Shots

As a CEO, you don't want to be told what to do. I get it. I've been an entrepreneur since I was seventeen, so I can pull the levers and command my own ship. Compliance is really irritating because we're told by state and federal regulators and insurance companies how to run our businesses. They slap ten pages of rules on our desks and say, "Do this or else."

In response, a lot of executives find a way to disown the responsibility of compliance. I've heard all kinds of excuses from clients about why compliance isn't a priority.

"I'm too small. No one is coming after *me*."

"I'll just buy this tool and then I'm compliant."

"What will it cost if I *don't* do that and get caught?"

"I don't have to worry about hackers because I have cyber insurance."

Sure, you can choose to go on thinking like that. There's no such thing as the Compliance Police doing spot checks and passing out tickets if you don't follow HIPAA (or other regulations) to the letter. Like Joe's dad, you can speed along for some time with relatively few issues. But the reason why Joe's story is important—and what I need CEOs to understand—is that when it comes to being compliant in your business, problems and consequences appear *after* an incident.

Joe's history of speeding and not complying with simple laws didn't start when he was sixteen. He learned as a child that he didn't have to pay attention to the speed limit signs.

As a leader, all eyes are on you. If you break the law, your employees will follow, and you'll have an organization-wide culture of noncompliance. When you get breached (because you will), it will cost you a lot more.

All Eyes Are on You

We know that employees are the #1 vulnerability for companies. Human error causes 85% of all data breaches.[51] If you, the CEO, ignore the speed limit sign, employees will ignore the signs. If a CEO doesn't follow simple regulations, why would an employee care if they click on a phishing email or send personally identifiable information (PII) in an email?

When your employee unwittingly gives away login credentials to a hacker, investigators will show up with their microscopes. When willful disregard and negligence for the rules are at play, things get bad for CEOs, and punitive fines reach into millions of dollars. Like Joe, you'll nurse your scrapes and bruises, thinking, "Wait, I was hacked! I'm the victim here!" Unfortunately, compliance is your responsibility and yours alone.

Everyone else is holding YOU accountable, no matter who is at fault. Regulatory bodies, consumers, patients, investors, stakeholders, and employees expect businesses to protect their information.

Today, there's more PII out in the world than ever before. To get access to that valuable data, there's been a massive uptick in cyberthreat actors, and it's getting worse. In 2016, the average cost of a ransomware attack was $10,000. Today, it's $1 million.[52] Everyone is at risk of getting hacked—even the FBI, which is still investigating a hack discovered in early January 2023.[53] If even the FBI can't prevent itself from being hacked, what makes us CEOs think we can't (or won't) be hacked?

In response to this catastrophic increase in attacks, legislation is being passed by regulators moving away from a slap-on-the-wrist approach to more punitive action. They want executives to feel the weight of responsibility on their shoulders, so we're seeing more damaging lawsuits, penalties, and fines. Even jail time is being written into the new FTC safeguards as we speak. In 2022, the CISO of Uber was sentenced to three years' probation for covering up a data breach involving millions of users' records.

You aren't immune. No one is.

Compliance Is Simple, but It Starts with You

The role of leaders and executives in compliance is to be a positive example for their company. The easiest way to do that is to establish compliance as a culture. Compliance as a culture means that every action taken by an employee in your organization is done with security in mind. It's not an afterthought—it's a proactive plan with built-in accountability.

Just like "Speed Limit 65" signs, compliance is simple. But as with a speed limit sign, you must also follow it for it to protect you. Compliance plans take it one step further by requiring you to prove that you follow the rules. This benefits you because when a drunk driver slams into you—i.e., a hacker steals your data—you must prove to investigators that you are compliant and proactively protecting your business and customer data.

When I work with clients, we help them develop a culture of compliance in three phases. First, we establish a mission and vision around compliance and security. Next, we identify which frameworks they need to adhere to, such as HIPAA, NIST, PCI, etc. The last thing we do is develop internal policies and procedures to follow the framework consistently and ensure a paper trail proves that all the processes are followed.

1. Establish Your Vision

"Each and every customer impacted is one too many." That's what Kaseya CEO Fred Voccola said in response to his company's data breach in 2021. Their vision is clear:

A breach should never impact their customers. It's a hard line in the sand, but that vision has a lot to do with the success of Kaseya's breach remediation and should be a goal for every company.

Kaseya is an IT and security software vendor for MSPs like me, and I remember getting updates and emails every hour throughout the entire process. They were swift to initiate their rapid remediation and mitigation plan. In the end, only fifty of Kaseya's 35,000 customers were breached. It could've been worse, but like clockwork, investigators showed up. Instead of sweating through their button-down shirts, Kaseya worked with the FBI, CISA, the Department of Homeland Security, and the White House to resolve the breach. Kaseya wasn't fined. There were no penalties, no jail time. Why? Because they were compliant, they had a plan, and they followed through. The FBI special agent in charge of the cyber division during the investigation was so impressed with Kaseya's response to the breach that he left the FBI to become chief information security officer at Kaseya.[54]

Your vision can be as simple as "We're not letting a low-life hacker take us down." We will follow the speed limit signs because that's what will keep us running. It protects jobs, pays paychecks, and supports our growing businesses. Your vision for compliance must be something you feel comfortable speaking about at every team meeting. Don't check boxes behind closed office doors; make what you're doing visible and talk about it all the time.

2. Identify Your Framework

Once your vision is clear, the next step is to identify which compliance framework(s) you need. Almost every business dealing with credit cards must be PCI compliant (though most aren't), but some need to adhere to multiple compliance frameworks. For example, if you're a medical office accepting credit cards, you're dealing with PCI and HIPAA compliance.

Your framework also depends on your customer base. Are you a law firm that does personal injury cases? That's HIPAA. It's the same for my MSP. We serve medical practices, so I must be HIPAA compliant. Many SMBs don't realize that, and it makes them incredibly vulnerable.

I tell clients that even if their business isn't required to comply with federal regulations, they should follow a security framework like NIST, especially as more states pass safe harbor laws. My home state of Utah has safe harbor laws that say that if you are compliant and experience a breach, your business has extra protection from litigation. Utah, Connecticut, and Ohio passed safe harbor laws in the last few years, and several others plan to follow suit. If you deploy a compliance framework, these laws grant you additional layers of vital protection.

3. Develop Consistent Internal Systems

How often do you tell your kids to clean their room? Is it once a year at the end of the year? On December 31, do you say, "Did you clean your room? Well, do it next year." No. If you want your kids to pick up their socks and put their toys away, you remind them every day. If they don't do it, do you just let their stuff pile up until you can't see their bedroom floor? No, you probably put some consequences in place.

In the same way, the key to implementing a successful compliance culture is to make it as easy and consistent as possible AND to hold your team accountable. You can't slap a rulebook on the table and tell your company, "Here's my vision: follow this." That's not a culture of compliance. That's just conforming to a government document. Internal systems involve repeated cybersecurity awareness training with your team, ongoing simulated phishing tests, and regular monitoring and penetration testing. Implement strategies that track security progress and have repercussions for those who don't pull their weight.

Have your internal IT department deploy the framework or outsource it to a managed security services provider. Whatever support you enlist, your processes must be recurring and involve regular follow-through because THAT builds a thriving culture of compliance and security in your business.

Top-down Compliance Keeps Your Foot on the Gas

You are going to get breached at some point. No tool, software, or service is going to save you. But if you have a culture of compliance when you are breached, what will the results be? How is the media going to see you? How are your staff and clients going to see you? When compliance is a top-down culture in your company, not only will you be seen more like Kaseya and less like Uber, but the ancillary benefits are endless.

A top-down compliance culture builds trust and confidence in your business among employees, customers, and stakeholders who see you as a reliable and responsible partner. Companies that regularly test their incident response plan save an average of $2.6 million after a breach,[55] meaning you'll bounce back much faster. If you aren't leading your team with a strong compliance mindset, you will miss out on opportunities to grow at scale, attract investors, earn customer loyalty, and recruit and retain the best talent on the market. If you react to breaches instead of planning for them, it will slam on the brakes of your business, forcing you to a dead stop. Maybe for good.

We all want to drive fast like Joe and his dad. We like to feel the G-forces push us back in our seats as we skyrocket our growth and profits. When compliance rolls up like a concrete speed bump, we're tempted to speed over it. However, when we embrace compliance as a culture, it seamlessly integrates into everything we do. It becomes a driving force that empowers us to thrive and grow instead of bringing us to a screeching stop. While other businesses are colliding with hackers and nursing their wounds and going out of business, your organization will be resilient, with your foot pressed firmly on the gas.

About Gregory

Like many tech innovators, Greg Mauer's love of technology started with a computer game. From building better computers to networking multiple computers so he could play with friends, a love of technology was solidified early on in Greg's life. By the time he was seventeen in 1997, he had founded his own company.

Just like most IT professionals at the time, Greg started his business under the break-fix model. However, as technology advanced during the mid-2000s, he realized its limitations and transitioned his business model to a managed services provider. His decision to make this shift was driven by frustration with being called in after a network stopped working or a hacker ransomed a business's data—after the damage was already done. He recognized the real value in proactive measures, maintenance, monitoring, and fine-tuning to ensure the reliability and security of his clients' systems.

After serving hundreds of clients across the greater Salt Lake City, Utah, region, Greg believes the industry still has substantial room for improvement. Although modern organizations have embraced technology, they often fail to prioritize a crucial fundamental aspect of their operation—cybersecurity.

Greg aims to change this narrative by engaging in high-level discussions with clients, ensuring that every decision made at the executive level considers security and compliance, and leaving the outdated perception of "IT is just a line item on the budget" in the past. Greg is constantly on the cutting edge of security and compliance, initiating business conversations and risk assessments while elevating the role of cybersecurity professionals from button pushers to indispensable advisors who actively contribute to strategic business decisions.

Outside of his role as CEO of qnectU, Greg cherishes his personal life, finding joy and fulfillment as a husband, father, and aviator. An experienced pilot of more than two decades, Greg takes to the air every chance he can, relishing the freedom and exhilaration that flying brings. But lately, Greg and Rebecca, his wife of twenty-five years and business partner, have been busier than usual. Recently, they welcomed into their family a beautiful baby boy who enjoys spending much of his time with his working parents in their office. Alongside their family is a loyal one-hundred-pound Rottweiler, who faithfully accompanies the family on their many adventures.

For more information, contact Greg at qnectU:

Email: greg@qnectu.com
Phone: (801) 572-4000
Web: www.qnectu.com
LinkedIn: www.linkedin.com/in/gregory-e-mauer-qnectu

WHY IT'S A DANGEROUS MISTAKE TO DUMP THE ENTIRE BURDEN OF COMPLIANCE ON YOUR INTERNAL IT DEPARTMENT

Tim Conard

The IT industry is very much like the construction industry . . .

If you've got a building that needs to be built, you're not going to expect the roofer to do your electrical work, the electrician to do your plumbing, or the painter to do your concrete work. Each has a different and unique skill set.

The same goes for the IT industry . . .

You shouldn't expect your data analyst to handle all your cybersecurity needs, your software engineer to install new hardware on your network, or your web developer to maintain your software databases. Each has a different and unique skill set. *The same thing applies to compliance.* You shouldn't expect someone to handle your IT-related compliance requirements merely because they fall under the IT umbrella in your company. No IT person in this world knows everything about everything. There is just too much to learn and too many skill sets. Compliance requires specific skills, experience, and know-how.

There are many other issues to consider before you assign the compliance burden to your internal IT department. Here are twenty-two reasons why hiring an MSP to assist you with compliance makes good business sense:

1. **Improved communication.** I've found that the IT aspect represents only about 40% of compliance. Compliance involves the policies and procedures of the entire organization. It's a team effort. Compliance requirements involve multiple departments, including legal, finance, human resources, and operations. To manage the "other 60%" of compliance, a company employee takes on the role of compliance officer. It's critical to have excellent communication between the IT compliance team and the compliance officer. An MSP is well-trained at communicating with management and compliance officers about all compliance aspects in easy-to-understand, "nontech-speak" terms. Whereas, if you rely on your internal IT department, they must develop a new skill set.

2. **Expertise.** From a technical perspective, internal IT people are limited to their environment. Their focus is on maintaining stability in their environment. MSPs experience a lot of different environments on an ongoing basis. They are regularly exposed to many situations and innovations in the industry, whereas internal IT departments that aren't co-managed only see and experience significant changes every three to five years. The internal IT department focuses on keeping up with the company's daily operations. An MSP has specialized expertise and experience in compliance that many companies lack internally.

3. **Cost efficiency.** An MSP spreads its compliance-related costs (training, certifications, resource investment, staff) over multiple clients. MSPs take advantage of economies of scale and can offer IT-related compliance services for less than it would take to build and maintain the same in-house expertise.

4. **Software access.** There are a lot of technology companies that will not sell their software directly to internal IT departments. For example, our business continuity disaster recovery solutions—the best on the market—cannot be purchased unless you're an MSP. This is because those companies want to work with people who understand their technology.

5. **The latest compliance-related innovations.** An internal IT person's day is generally filled with taking care of employees and what needs to be done in their IT environment. Typically, they do not have time to research the latest marketplace innovation. An MSP stays on top of constantly changing regulations and compliance best practices and will communicate any pertinent changes and information to your company's compliance officer.

6. **Continuous monitoring.** Running remote management and monitoring solutions is pretty much a full-time job if you want to do it effectively. Many smaller IT departments don't have the resources or expertise to manage all the data and information about every system. An MSP typically operates on a 24/7 basis, which allows them to monitor all their clients' systems continuously. Plus, they have access to advanced tools that make them aware of issues before they become serious problems.

7. **Centralized management.** An MSP centralizes the management of your IT infrastructure. This makes it easier to monitor compliance-related activities. It reduces the time and resources required to manage compliance internally, which can result in cost savings.

8. **Improved outcomes.** Studies have shown that outsourcing complex functions like compliance can lead to better results and performance. A compliance-focused MSP has the expertise to understand and stay current on all the regulations and quickly identify and address potential risks. They also can provide a tailored solution that meets your industry-specific compliance requirements.

9. **Compliance best practices.** Best practices are defined as "a standard or set of guidelines known to produce the best outcomes if followed." An MSP's profitability depends upon how efficiently, effectively, and economically they work within whatever environment they are managing. To achieve maximum profitability, best practices are followed in everything they do, including compliance. Because of their limited experience, an internal IT department may not be aware of compliance best practices.

10. **Reduced IT department workload.** Outsourcing compliance lets your internal IT team focus on other priorities. This reduction in workload can also improve their work-life balance. Often, IT people are overworked and overwhelmed and have no one to back them up. If something goes wrong, they are the ones who get the call in the middle of the night. What if they're on vacation or have a sick day? When they have an MSP, whether on a co-managed or fully outsourced basis, you don't have to worry because there's an entire team supporting your business, not just one or two people. Plus, MSPs leverage advanced automation tools to manage and monitor compliance in your infrastructure. This frees up your internal IT staff to work on

more strategic projects. In addition, it reduces the MSP's labor investment, which means they can provide their services to you at a highly competitive price point.

11. **Objectivity.** Sometimes, internal IT departments add unnecessary complexity to your environment to justify their existence, protecting their jobs because they are the only ones with tribal knowledge or the "keys to the kingdom." It pains me to write this, but I've seen it firsthand. They don't realize that by engaging with an MSP in a co-managed relationship, they will not only become better engineers, but the company they work for will benefit greatly, which would protect their jobs. An MSP's only agenda is to make your company compliant as efficiently and cost-effectively as possible.

12. **Risk reduction.** Because of an MSP's experience with a wide variety of compliance scenarios, they will do a more thorough, accurate analysis and compliance implementation than someone new to the ins and outs of compliance requirements. This also means they can identify and remediate potential risks early on, which reduces the risk of fines and penalties that result from noncompliance.

13. **Cost reduction.** I often say that every IT fix is a fifteen-minute fix . . . *if you know what to do.* If you don't know what you're doing, you'll probably spend twenty to thirty times that amount of time educating yourself about the problem and how to remediate it. Compliance can take a lot more time than it should when done by someone tasked with doing it once vs. an MSP with experience doing it multiple times.

14. **Flexibility and scalability.** An MSP can quickly adapt if compliance requirements change. They will allocate additional resources or outsource additional support from one of their trusted partners if necessary. Internal IT departments that don't have specific relationships established often roll the dice and do an online search for what they need and hire a company they have no track record with.

15. **Faster adaption to change.** Greek philosopher Heraclitus once said, "The only constant in life is change." Compliance requirements are constantly evolving. When it's not their primary focus, it can be challenging for an internal IT department to monitor and react to changes quickly. Plus, adding a specific type of improvement to a product or service may put your company

at an entirely different compliance level. This can lead to noncompliance, resulting in penalties, fines, and other legal consequences.

16. **End-user education.** Ninety-five percent of breaches come from someone clicking on something they shouldn't have. An MSP will have a proven comprehensive user-education program. With an internal IT person, one person might go around to everybody in the company warning them what not to click on, but that is inconsistent and incomplete.

17. **Documentation and reporting.** With compliance, everything must be thoroughly documented to demonstrate compliance to regulators and auditors. An MSP will ensure your documentation and reporting are correct, saving you time and ensuring your documents are always accurate and current.

18. **Competing priorities.** Internal IT people are often stretched in multiple directions within a company. Management in one department wants their project done ASAP. And so does management in another department. The priority that wins out might be chosen because it puts the IT person in the best light and/or allows them to keep their job.

19. **Increased IT awareness.** When you bring in a third-party vendor because they have had different experiences and training, there's a good chance they will open your IT department up to new ideas, viewpoints, and a better way of doing things moving forward.

20. **Cyber insurance coverage.** When applying for cybersecurity insurance, the insurance company sends you a self-assessment questionnaire (SAQ) to fill out. All too often, a C-level manager pencil whips the form and sends it back. Should you have a breach, the insurance company will verify that everything you said on the SAQ is accurate. If it's not, they will deny your claim. An MSP has experience filling out these SAQs and will fill them out accurately, with the assistance of management, so you'll never have any issues should you need to make a claim. When you get coverage, be extremely clear about what the insurance company will cover and what they will not. For instance, some insurance companies don't cover ransomware payments or related damage from a ransomware attack. An MSP can help you determine the type of coverage and policy you need for your business.

21. **Regular audits and assessments.** Compliance is not a "one-and-done" situation. It's an ongoing commitment. An MSP will perform regular audits and

assessments in coordination with other company departments to ensure your business environment remains compliant. Plus, regular audits and assessments allow you to discuss how to improve and proactively solve problems.

22. **Access to trusted partners.** If an MSP doesn't offer a specific skill set, most will contact one of their trusted partners to help you meet your goals. This gives you access to specialized expertise, streamlined vendor management, and potential cost savings, as often MSPs give each other preferential pricing because of their ongoing relationship.

You have an IT department, so you and your business can focus on what you do best: selling your products and services. The above twenty-two reasons are why your IT department should be allowed to focus on what they do best: designing, maintaining, and managing your company's technology infrastructure—and why leaving your compliance requirements to someone who lives and breathes it daily makes sense.

About Tim

Tim Conard founded TS Conard Inc. Technology Solutions, based in St. Joseph, Missouri, in August 2003. They
provide IT and compliance solutions to businesses in north-
western Missouri and northeast Kansas, focusing on companies with twenty-plus employees in the manufacturing,
small government, transportation, and financial sectors.
Tim initially started his business as a software development

company, but people kept asking if TS Conard could fix their computers. Recogniz-
ing the need in his community, Tim quickly switched the mandate of his company to
fulfill the growing demand for IT services and expertise.

Tim's ability to adapt to an ever-changing environment can be traced back to his
time in the US Marines. On August 17, 1987, three days after his seventeenth birthday, he enlisted with the Marines—a dream he had had since he was five years old. He
served with the sixty-seven elite marines of the Marine Detachment aboard the USS
Forrestal for two years and seven months, where he rose to the rank of corporal. In his
last nine months of service, Tim transferred to the Weapons Company, 3rd Battalion,
6th Marine Regiment, where he completed his third deployment. He uses the key
attributes he learned as a marine (discipline and resilience, leadership skills, teamwork
and camaraderie, problem-solving and decision-making, core values and ethics) and
fine-tuned them to become the leader and person he is today.

The best part of Tim's day-to-day work life as president of TS Conard is educating
clients and potential clients on their IT and compliance requirements and seeing the
proverbial light bulb go off above their heads. While Tim is motivated to get up each
morning by the prospect of helping his clients achieve all their IT and compliance
goals, it's much bigger than that. Tim sees his role and that of the team at TS Conard
as being a positive force that helps strengthen communities. Tim knows that if he can
help businesses become more efficient, effective, economical, and profitable, they'll
hire more people, strengthening the community's employment base and adding to
its prosperity.

Tim sits on several boards, including the Southside Development Corporation
Board, and was part of St. Joseph's Capital Improvement Campaign Committee. He
enjoys public speaking through the local Chamber of Commerce. Tim has given talks
that inform businesses about cybersecurity, compliance, and how they can better pro-

tect their employees, customers, and data. He is a Missouri Western State University graduate with bachelor's degrees in computer science and computer information systems. He actively volunteers in his community and loves working with nonprofits to help them grow and significantly impact their community.

For more information, contact Tim at TS Conard:

    Email: tim@tsconard.com
    Phone: (816) 542-3189
    Web: www.tsconard.com

Chapter 14

WHY YOU HAVE NO CHOICE BUT TO BE HONEST ABOUT YOUR CYBER HYGIENE
Rick Rudolph

L et's get personal for a minute. Have you been neglecting your hygiene? Your cyber hygiene, that is. Chances are you have, considering that 88% of Americans report that they take necessary steps to stay safe from cyberattacks, but less than half actually perform the bare minimum when it comes to cyber hygiene.[56] Maybe that's because many small and medium business owners don't know what *cyber hygiene* is.

To put it simply, cyber hygiene is a set of routine practices that a company puts in place to protect its network and assets from cyberthreats, ensure you get the best performance from all your connected devices, and help detect computer problems before they become problems.

While a basic cyber hygiene checklist might look simple—with common-sense best practices like keeping devices patched, not sharing credentials, using strong passwords, implementing multifactor authentication, performing regular backups, and installing antivirus and malware software—don't get comfortable thinking it's the be-all and end-all solution for battling cybersecurity risks. These are just the building blocks of an exhaustive cybersecurity strategy that can help reduce the security gaps that cybercriminals can take advantage of.

Why Good Cyber Hygiene Is Nonnegotiable

Now that you know what cyber hygiene is, why does it matter so much? Because technology is the driving force behind every business, and without it, there's almost

ZERO chance you can manage your daily operations.

I started my career as a CPA back in 1980, so I had the luxury of seeing how businesses were run before computers were a workforce thing. I would visit clients' offices, and they would have fifty to sixty people just on their accounting staff. Now, these same companies have two or three people manning their accounting offices, and it's all about technology. While technology reduces the impact of human error, eliminates repetitive tasks, gives us access to real-time data, improves compliance, increases revenue, and offers many other benefits, it also introduces risk. Hardware and software failure, human error, spam, viruses, and malicious attacks. Just as the benefits of technology have changed the way we do business, so have the threats.

It wasn't so long ago when businesses didn't need to worry about cyber hygiene. Computers were locked in a room where nobody was allowed in unless they wore a white coat and had some impressive credentials on their name tags. It was like a medieval method of security. You had a castle surrounded by a moat, surrounded by a wall, and the only access was a drawbridge. Back then, you could see when threats approached, so you kept the drawbridge up. But that way of doing business disappeared with the Internet, and now the criminals have figured out sophisticated ways of piercing the fortress before you even know what's hit you.

Today, a typical SMB IT infrastructure is a complex weave of physical servers, cloud computing processes, databases, desktop and laptop computers, software applications, and mobile devices. Every access point connected to the Internet is a target for cyberattacks. Businesses can't let their guard down when it comes to improving their cyber hygiene. It takes a solid commitment from the C-suite to defend against today's cybersecurity threats.

Why else is good cyber hygiene important? Without it, you'll have a difficult time getting a cybersecurity insurance policy—at least one you can afford.

Cyber Policies and Your Cyber Hygiene Score

If your business handles customer data or stores information about your business online, then cybersecurity insurance is a MUST. This is just a fact. And don't think because you're not a large enterprise that cyber attackers aren't coming after you—they're actually targeting you. In the first quarter of 2023 alone, one in thirty-one organizations worldwide experienced a ransomware attack weekly.[57] And 60% of small businesses that get hacked close their doors within six months after an attack.[58] Still don't think you need cybersecurity insurance?

So, just what is cybersecurity insurance, and what does it cover? It's a policy that protects your business against financial losses caused by incidents like data breaches, ransomware extortion demands, theft, and system hacking. Cyber insurance can also help with the fees and expenses associated with notifying customers about a breach, restoring their identities, and recovering compromised data. But here's the thing. Cyber insurance is not cheap.

Depending on your coverage options, cyber policies can range in annual costs anywhere from $500 to $5,000 and up. There are several factors that can influence the price, but one important one is your cyber hygiene "score."

Insurers will use an underwriting questionnaire to assess the level of security of your organization's networks and systems. Think of it like a credit score. Instead of lenders using the information to determine whether you get a mortgage, credit card, or some other line of credit, a cyber hygiene score lets insurance companies determine how vulnerable your business is to cyberattacks and whether or not you are worth the risk.

A few years ago, you could expect the underwriting questionnaire to be just a few basic questions like "How often do you change your passwords?" and "Do you have a backup system in place?" But now they're much more comprehensive and complex. That's because insurers have paid out a LOT of money over the last few years as attacks surge. Their loss ratio averaged 49% between 2015 and 2022, which is why cyber insurance premiums have increased upward of 50%.[59]

Back to the questionnaire. Every insurer will have their own assessment, and different industries, like defense and health care or publicly traded companies, will have different standards and compliance questions, but most business owners can expect to provide in-depth answers about the types of data you work with, network security, payment card, content liability, and vendor controls you have in place. You'll have to answer questions about the types of disaster recovery and incident response plans you have. They'll want to know about your outsourced services, any previous computer system disruptions from an attack or a failure, and lots more. It's not a fun process.

When you answer "yes" that you have these plans and controls in place, your cybersecurity hygiene score is favorable. You can answer "no" to a question or questions and an insurer might decline you outright, or they might still write you a policy, but your premiums will likely be outrageously expensive.

Keep in mind that this underwriting questionnaire is an affidavit. If you say you're doing something, you better be doing it. If you're not and you get hit, they're going to send in a forensics team before they ever write a check. If they find out you lied or misled them, they'll deny your claim and walk away. It's a lose-lose situation if you're paying the premiums but end up losing the money because you lied.

Know Where You Stand Before You Reach Out to an Insurer

Before you go about trying to find the best-priced cyber coverage, you need to have good security measures in place to help lower your risk exposure and make you a stronger candidate for coverage. That starts with a basic audit of your business's current IT landscape. Here are some of the bare-minimum cyber hygiene measures you can assess for yourself:

- **Multifactor authentication.** Are we using and requiring everyone to implement multifactor authentication to confirm their identity before accessing the network, systems, or applications?
- **Endpoint protection.** Do we have the proper endpoint protection tools in place for all desktops, laptops, smartphones, tablet computers, and other connected devices?
- **Endpoint detection and response.** Are we continuously monitoring end-user devices to detect and respond to cyberthreats like ransomware and malware?
- **Email security.** Are we protecting users and their email with anti-spam and anti-phishing technology?
- **Modern firewall.** Is our firewall a next-gen firewall that is regularly updated to detect and prevent intrusions?
- **Backups.** Are we backing up our important data and doing it frequently, using external media and a secure cloud service? Are we doing regular test restores?
- **Access rights and permissions.** Do only authorized individuals have user accounts, and are they granted only as much access or permission as necessary to perform their job?

Again, these are the basic measures you need to have in place. The next step is to implement the necessary tools and technology that can close the security gaps, strengthen your cybersecurity defenses against the most severe risks, and prove you have the processes in place to qualify for cyber insurance. To help you do that, it's critical to have an expert third-party IT security partner in your corner.

For IT services providers like myself, it's easy to see if a business is doing what they need to be doing to protect themselves from cyberthreats. It's like driving by someone's yard—you know immediately whether or not the grass is being mowed. Looking at a business's network is no different when you know what you are looking for. Believe me, I know cybersecurity isn't a fun or sexy part of doing business. But it is fundamentally crucial and requires expert knowledge. Even for businesses with their own internal IT department, employees are often overwhelmed with everyday responsibilities and have no specialized training in cybersecurity.

Here are a few more detailed assessments a good third-party provider can do to help decrease your chances of being declined by insurers and increase your potential cyber hygiene score—which can mean lower premiums to pay and more money in your pocket.

1. Review the security policies you have in place.
2. Identify your assets, threats, and vulnerabilities and analyze their risks.
3. Assess risks, their likelihood, and the impact they would have on your business.
4. Document the risks.
5. Decide how your business will manage or mitigate risks that are identified.
6. Determine when you will avoid, accept, or insure residual risks.

You Can't Rely on Cyber Insurance—or Hygiene—Alone

Don't let having a cyber insurance policy give you a false sense of security. And the fact that maybe you have an A++ cyber hygiene score—good for you—doesn't mean anything if you set-it-and-forget-it. There's always a possibility of a zero-day threat—an attack that no one's ever seen before, so they've never prepared for it. They happen every day. And while you might think your cybersecurity programs are 98% effective, in today's high-stakes cyberwarfare environment, it's the 2% gap that will come back and blow up in your face. Cybercriminals don't care how hard you tried.

No matter what your cybersecurity strategy is, it has to be continuous, as risks and business environments change way too often these days. You need to count on round-the-clock managed cybersecurity that's awake even when you or your teams aren't.

Conclusion

Though cyber insurance buyers are seeing smaller rate increases in 2023, businesses can still expect strict underwriting control requirements as the demand for new policies increases. And for SMBs diligently working toward a strong cybersecurity posture, cyber insurers have a lot to offer in supporting a business's efforts to recover after a cyberattack, including helping you evaluate your risk level to determine the type of coverage that's right for your business because there is no one-size-fits-all policy. What they don't offer is managed cybersecurity support.

A qualified IT services provider can implement the cybersecurity solutions you need to optimize your network and monitor your systems around the clock. And they can help you fill out your underwriting questionnaire—honestly and accurately—to help increase your chances of getting cyber insurance.

About Rick

Rick Rudolph is the founder and president of Solve, Ltd. He founded the Reston, Virginia-based firm thirty-two years ago to provide comprehensive IT services throughout the Mid-Atlantic region.

Solve, Ltd. specializes in outsourced IT support needs, including managed IT services, application development, disaster recovery planning, and cybersecurity to keep critical business systems operational twenty-four hours a day, seven days a week.

Rick's understanding and appreciation of security comes from his upbringing as an Air Force brat. His father was a B-52 pilot, so the family often lived in facilities that housed nuclear weapons.

Rick started his career as a CPA shortly after graduating from university. In his role as an accountant and auditor, he tested financial controls, which is uniquely similar to working around cybersecurity. After three years, he would become the CFO of a large building supply company where he supervised not only the accounting and financial departments but the information systems departments as well.

At age thirty-two, Rick founded a business consulting practice, which quickly morphed into a business dedicated to supporting IT for all different types of businesses in the Mid-Atlantic. By 1995, his company was designing, implementing, and managing secure wide-area networks (WANs) with a mission to provide the most appropriate technology solutions to each operational challenge their clients had while securing their data. Solve, Ltd. still adheres to those guiding principles today.

Over the past twenty years, Rick has been active in a number of MSP industry organizations whose primary focus is to "proactively" manage networked devices as opposed to a traditional ad hoc "break-fix" model. Hard-coded into today's environment, one cannot be "proactive" and provide high device availability without focusing first and foremost on securing the environment and providing for disaster recovery in the event of a successful breach. Rick currently spends a substantial amount of his time ensuring that his clients do not experience a catastrophic attack.

For more information, contact Rick at Solve, Ltd.:

Email: rrudolph@solveltd.com
Phone: (703) 879-2070
Web: www.solveltd.com
LinkedIn: www.linkedin.com/in/rickrudolph

Chapter 15

WHY CYBERSECURITY WON'T SAVE YOU IF YOU'RE NOT COMPLIANT

Jarom Renfeldt

'm from California, and I get it. As a business owner and leader, you feel over-burdened by laws and regulations. Your business focus is to market and sell your products and services, not jump through the hoops established by the various compliance regulatory agencies. Besides, you have an IT team or an IT person who handles all your IT requirements. Isn't that enough?

It's not. While every company needs to focus on cybersecurity, compliance is the cost of doing business in today's cyber-hacker-saturated environment. Cybersecurity measures are essential, but keeping your data safe without compliance standards and controls is a murky gray area. You might think about it occasionally, but then again, you might not. Compliance gives you an actual structure—a best practices framework that will reduce your chances of being the victim of a cyberattack. The following are seven areas where cybersecurity alone won't save you but being compliant will.

1. Recovery Plan

If your company gets breached, here are three basic steps your IT person most likely will attempt to do: 1) kick the cyber attacker out; 2) fix all the problems and the damage the cyber attacker created—usually, this involves restoring your data from a backup; and 3) take steps to prevent the cyber attacker from getting in again. Common sense, right? The primary goal is to get your company up and running again, and these steps will accomplish that.

However, there's an enormous problem. Step two is *not* legal. If you simply restore your data from a backup, you're also erasing the forensics that tell you what data was stolen and who stole it. *If your business has not made any effort to be compliant, you might not know this and would unknowingly be breaking the law.* You must have a forensic company come in to evaluate the situation, figure out what data has been compromised, and put together a report of their findings. This could take days, weeks, and sometimes even months. Meanwhile, as time passes, your business is suffering and may never recover.

This is why engaging a third party specializing in compliance is crucial to helping you meet your compliance requirements. Security is unique to every organization, and the application of the compliance standards must be customized to the structure and posture of the organization. During a breach, the first thing a compliance specialist will do is have you engage a local forensic company they know and trust. The forensic company will familiarize themselves with your setup so they'll be ready to respond quickly in case of a breach. If your business suffers a breach, an MSP/MSSP will be monitoring your network and will kick out the cyber attacker immediately. Then they will get the forensic company involved. The forensic company will be able to quickly determine what data has been breached, and the MSP/MSSP will get you back up and running. Instead of days or weeks, your business will be back up and running in as little as a couple of hours.

2. Legal Ramifications

Regulations are a set of standards and rules adopted by administrative agencies. While they are technically not laws, they often have the same force as laws because if they didn't, the regulatory agencies would not be able to enforce them. In our society, we have laws and rules for general safety that protect us from each other, organizations, and the government itself. We have laws overseeing the safety of our food and roads, laws that protect us from discrimination, and so on. It makes sense that we would have regulations to keep your data and business safe from foreign intruders and malice.

In California, there is something called the California Consumer Privacy Act that most businesses must comply with. (Note: Many other states have regulations that are equivalent to the CCPA. If your state doesn't, you are under the jurisdiction of federal compliance regulations.) I've talked to companies that were under the impression that if they don't sell directly to consumers, the compliance regulations don't apply to them. This is incorrect. Information on consumers falls under personally identifiable information. If you have employees, you have PII. This means you must be compliant with the CCPA (or your state's equivalent regulations).

So, where cybersecurity is the protection of computer systems, networks, and data from unauthorized access, attacks, and damage, compliance is a framework of regulations, standards, and policies that have been established and must be followed to ensure your data remains safe. It involves implementing policies and procedures that govern data retention, access controls, encryption, user consent, and secure data handling. Plus, while a business can say they are taking the necessary cybersecurity protection measures, compliance is *proof* that they are doing so.

What is this proof saving you from? If you are breached, under the CCPA, civil penalties go up to $2,500 per record of the violation. (With an intentional violation—a violation where you're aware of the requirements but choose not to comply— the penalty can increase to $7,500 per violation.) So, if you've violated the rights of thousands upon thousands of consumers, and each consumer had dozens of records compromised, this can add up quickly. In some states, individuals are allowed to sue companies that lose their data. So, depending upon what state the breach occurs in, it could open you up to class action lawsuits. Lose one class action lawsuit and your business may never recover. Plus, you may be ordered to pay for long-term credit monitoring for all the people who had their data breached.

If that's not devastating enough for your business, consider this: If your business is breached and your data is compromised, depending upon what state you do business in, you must report it to the appropriate authorities, notify your state's attorney general, and/or notify media outlets. A data breach can severely impact your company's brand reputation. Consumers and vendors may no longer trust you, investors might shun you, and employee morale could take a hit, making it challenging to keep valued employees and hire qualified new employees.

If you're the leader of a business, you'll want to be especially aware of the following: Previously, if your business got compromised, you could basically "pass the buck" to your IT person and say it's all their fault. That's all changed in the last two years or so. They've made it so *owners or company leaders can no longer be absolved by throwing up their hands and saying they weren't aware of the situation. As a leader, you are accountable for your IT department's mistakes, knowingly or unknowingly. Ignoring or failing to report a breach has severe government penalties and, more recently, even jail time for the business leader.*

3. Cybersecurity Insurance

If you're not compliant, chances are you will not be able to buy cybersecurity insurance to help you mitigate the costs should you be hacked. Not having cybersecurity insurance can cost you dearly when you consider an IBM report found that, in 2022, the average cost of a business data breach was $9.44 million.

If, when filling out the policy application form, you check "Yes" when the correct answer is "No" and provide other inaccurate information, the insurance company will not pay out, which could have disastrous financial results for your company. Many insurance companies require a third-party audit within the past year and a half before agreeing to insure you. According to NetworkAssured.com, in the past three years, cyber insurance claims have increased by 100% and payouts by 200%.

It's important to note that cybersecurity insurance will not cover any government fines or civil penalties associated with a breach.

4. It's Not Just About Your Business Anymore

In Target's famous 2013 data breach, the attackers got into Target's corporate network by compromising a third-party vendor, a refrigeration contractor by the name of Fazio Mechanical. One of Fazio's employees had clicked on a phishing email. A banking trojan was installed, and hackers were able to get Fazio Mechanical's login credentials.

When it comes to compliance and protecting your business from cyber attackers, you are no longer accountable just for your company's actions. To keep your data safe, it has become a necessity that compliance standards be "flowed down" (i.e., extended) from one party to another in a contractual relationship. In other words, your business should only buy from a company you know is compliant. This is a challenge—especially with US defense contractors—because often there is a deep line of subcontractors and suppliers behind every product their contractors produce. However, even entrusting sensitive data to third parties introduces additional risks. Compliance flow-down clauses ensure that every business involved in the supply chain complies with relevant laws, regulations, and industry standards. The goal is to hold all parties accountable to meet their regulatory obligations and foster a culture of compliance throughout the supply chain, maintaining a secure ecosystem.

A phishing attack is the most common way for a company to be breached. A phishing attack is an email requesting money—and the email looks like it came from someone in your company. When a company gets breached, cyber attackers will get into your email account and send emails to all your clients and vendors pretending to be you. One strategy is to inform your client that you've changed your banking account routing number and other contact information. Then the cyber attacker gives them their routing number and information. The next time the client makes a payment, the money is sent to the cyber attacker. When this happens, even if it's caught and rectified immediately, clients and vendors will suddenly be nervous about doing business with you.

If you just focus on your internal cybersecurity and ignore the compliance status of your vendors, you are increasing the chances of your business being the victim of a cyberattack.

5. Risk Management

Compliance frameworks often emphasize risk management and the implementation of controls to mitigate identified risks. While cybersecurity measures are part of the risk management process, compliance requires a broader perspective. It entails establishing governance frameworks, internal controls, and risk assessment methodologies that go beyond technical aspects. Compliance helps organizations identify, assess, and manage risks systematically, ensuring that appropriate controls and measures are in place to protect against various threats, both internal and external.

6. Trust and Reputation

If your business is the target of a cyberattack, your company's reputation will take a huge hit. Some clients and prospects will no longer trust you to protect their data. (According to the 2022 Hiscox *Cyber Readiness Report*, 29% of US companies had increased difficulty attracting new customers after an attack.) Your business will fall under media and public scrutiny. The negative headlines can linger in people's minds for years. You'll be the brunt of social media criticism and negative energy. And investors could shy away from your company. The National Cybersecurity Alliance reported that, as of 2021, 60% of small and medium-sized businesses went out of business within six months after a cyberattack.

In 2017, Equifax, a credit reporting company, was breached. Hackers broke in and stole 147 million records of people's private information. Equifax agreed to pay a settlement of $425 million to the Federal Trade Commission, the Consumer Financial Protection Bureau, and the fifty US states and territories. After news broke of their data breach, their shares plunged by about one-third. The hackers had gone unnoticed in Equifax's systems for more than six weeks, during which they meticulously extracted the data. In 2019, Equifax brought in a new leadership team and allocated over $1.25 billion to technology and security. While their reputation has recovered, they will always be associated with that data breach.

7. Employee Education

Educating your employees is a critical component of every cybersecurity strategy and is part of almost every compliance program. The importance of educating your employees can't be overstated because, according to the Verizon *2021 Data Breach Investigations Report*, 85% of successful data breaches involved human interaction, such as phishing emails or social engineering attacks. (Social engineering attacks include the hacker pretending to be a person of authority within the company, baiting someone with a free gift, or sending the victim to a malicious version of a legitimate website in hopes they will input sensitive data.) Part of the compliance service we offer clients is a comprehensive course in password hygiene, data protection policies, phishing prevention, and incident reporting procedures. This is so important that we don't give our clients the option to decline it. Instead, we require it and include it free of charge.

I've found that most companies that don't partner with an MSP/MSSP for their compliance requirements don't focus on educating their employees about compliance protection best practices. And if they do, it's done by an IT person who might not have the expertise needed in the cyberattack prevention area and spends just a few minutes with each employee going over what not to do.

Sadly, the bottom line is that cyber attackers are becoming so sophisticated and omnipresent that, eventually, every business will get breached. However, you can avoid downtime, the financial hit, having to negotiate with your cyber attackers, and damage to your reputation by ensuring that your business is compliant. Instead of thinking of it as a burden, think of it as gaining a competitive edge in the marketplace because noncompliant companies are starting to be left behind as more and more clients and vendors will do business with you only if you're compliant.

About Jarom

Jarom Renfeldt is the founder and president of Tech Guardian, a managed security services provider (MSSP) that partners with companies nationwide to help them become compliant. In April 2023, Tech Guardian earned its MSSP credentials—a major milestone for the company—something Jarom and the Tech Guardian team have been working on since 2001. An MSSP is a specialized type  of managed services provider that is specifically dedicated to security services. Besides the standard MSP security services, Tech Guardian offers more advanced services, such as threat intelligence (collecting and analyzing data to help you make better cybersecurity decisions) and threat hunting (searching for cyberthreats that may have already infiltrated a network but have not yet been detected by standard security systems).

Tech Guardian provides its clients with a "solution stack" comprised of top-tier security tools from the world's most highly rated and respected security companies. What sets Tech Guardian apart from many regular MSPs is that they are fully compliant themselves with the various compliance frameworks they work with, including PCI (Payment Card Industry), CIS (Center for Internet Security), HIPAA (Health Insurance Portability and Accountability Act), FTC Safeguards (financial sector compliance), and CMMC (Cybersecurity Maturity Model Certification). Plus, they are well-versed in each state's compliance laws to serve businesses in every state.

Involved with technology since he built his first computer at fifteen, Jarom has been in the IT industry for over twenty-seven years. At seventeen, he was working at Packard Bell doing tech support. Two years later, he was working for Microsoft. While attending college and touring different manufacturing companies, Jarom realized that small to medium-sized companies don't have nearly the level of technical sophistication that large companies do. So he started JR-Tech in his spare time.

Using a system called Smart Factory, he improved manufacturing companies' productivity by enabling communication with their computer-controlled machines. By the time he graduated, JR-Tech was a full-running company that helped manufacturing companies improve their cybersecurity in California's Inland Empire. In 2020, JR-Tech started offering compliance services. Jarom, who has an engineering degree from California State Polytechnical University's Pomona College of Engineering, uses the design engineering process to promote innovation, problem-solving, quality improvement, and more. In April 2023, upon becoming an MSSP, JR-Tech became Tech Guardian.

Jarom is the author of *Business IT 101: The Business Owner's Guide for Finding Hassle-Free Computer Support*, in which he educates business owners to leverage technology for competitive advantage and business growth. He is a member of top IT associations and is active in local and national IT communities.

Jarom has been a Boy Scout leader and mentor for fifteen years. He volunteers with Helping Our People in Elsinore (HOPE) and is active in the community through church and civic service. He is an action sports enthusiast, loves the outdoors, and, above all, enjoys spending time with his wife and four boys.

For more information, contact Jarom at Tech Guardian:

Email: jarom.renfeldt@tgmsp.com
Phone: (951) 319-4040
Web: www.techguardianmsp.com

Chapter 16
THE IMPACT OF NONCOMPLIANCE
Cora Park

Humans tend to avoid risk, especially when the value of what could be lost is high. We lock our doors every night, get guard dogs, and install security alarms to keep our families safe while we sleep. We set up doorbell cams to prevent holiday thieves from nabbing gifts off our porches, and we place fire extinguishers around our office to avoid fire damage. When what's at stake is high—our kids, dogs, home, property, and livelihood—we don't rely on luck to protect us. We spend money on layers of security to give us peace of mind.

Intruders, thieves, and fires—these are threats we're used to guarding against. But every year, the cyber world becomes more threatening. In 2021, 61% of small and midsize businesses (SMBs) were the target of a cyberattack.[60] It's no surprise that in 2022, industry leaders ranked cybersecurity as their #1 business risk.[61] But many SMBs still refuse to implement even basic protections, relying on good fortune and cyber insurance to protect them (it won't).

How We Got from "Mom-Dog-Run" to 115 Pages of Compliance

For a long time, you'd be okay with lax cybersecurity in your business. HIPAA was passed in 1996 when cybercrime was in its infancy, and hackers only broke into networks and systems to get hold of credit card numbers to commit smaller-scale identity theft. As little as three years ago, we recommended people use a random three-word passphrase like "mom-dog-run" as a strong password. Today, we discourage dictionary words. What worked then doesn't work now.

Cybercriminals today are often part of organized crime syndicates. The person on the other end of the phishing email is not just some guy in a hoodie sitting at a computer saying, "I'm going to hack Johnson's Pizza Shop." This is an organized crime enterprise with thousands of skilled, trained criminals, and you're sitting on a hotbed of data they can turn into cash. Even if you don't have credit cards or Social Security numbers, think about it—are you sitting on a fundraising email list with names, addresses, and email addresses? That's worth its weight in gold on the dark web, the unpoliced Wild West of the digital underworld, where criminals buy and sell stolen digital assets. It's only getting worse. In 2022, the average global data breach cost was $4.35 million, according to IBM's *Cost of a Data Breach Report 2022*. It was the highest in the seventeen-year history of IBM's report.[62] By 2025, global cybercrime is predicted to cost $10.5 trillion annually.[63] But many businesses are acting like it's 1998.

Not long ago, I asked a new client what password manager they used. Instead of showing me an app, my client reached into her purse and pulled out a metal ring with a thick block of index cards looped around it. On the index cards was every account username and password for the business. My jaw hit the floor. For her, it's easier to write it down and always have it on her person instead of logging into an app protected with multifactor authentication (MFA). This tactic might have passed fifteen years ago. But if she leaves that purse at a coffee shop or on a bench in the park, what do you think will happen?

Compliance Sucks

Cyber insurance providers and industry regulators like the US Department of Health and Human Services Office for Civil Rights (the entity that enforces HIPAA) and the bank that processes your credit cards (and enforces PCI DSS standards) know the odds of a business getting hacked are high. They require SMBs to meet specific security standards to protect the public—whose information is being stolen daily by the millions—keep money out of criminal hands and protect the businesses that drive our economy. When you meet those standards, it's called compliance.

Security tools don't come cheap, and investing in robust systems, firewalls, and encryption technologies to meet compliance standards can strain our financial resources. With so much else to think about, like hiring talent and scaling growth when running a business, many leaders don't reserve anything for compliance. You'll save yourself the effort, right?

Yeah, I hear you. Regulators suck, and compliance is confusing and expensive. There's no arguing that. But the cost of compliance isn't even close to the cost of noncompliance. Not by a long shot.

The Real Costs of Noncompliance

In a Ponemon Institute study of fifty-three multinational organizations, the average cost of compliance for organizations studied over one year was $5.47 million. However, direct and indirect costs of noncompliance—business disruption, legal fees, regulatory fines and penalties, and decreased productivity—are nearly three times higher at $14.82 million (though the range could be between $2.2 million to $39.22 million).[64] If you're noncompliant and suffer a cyberattack, you'll be paying a lot more than a ransom in your efforts to recover. It will cost you regulatory fines, your cyber insurance policy, customers, reputation, business opportunities, employees, or even your entire business.

Financial Losses

During the Colonial Pipeline hack in 2021, hackers got into the company's systems and sat undetected for weeks. The breach disrupted fuel supplies across the Southeastern United States. The company had not implemented multifactor authentication,[65] and criminals stole one password, allowing them access to the company's systems. It was all over the news for months and is constantly referenced as an example of what *not* to do in the security industry. You're thinking, *Yeah, but that's a massive company with a lot more money to attract hackers.* That's the thing—hackers attack SMBs using the same tactics as they do for larger companies. Thinking you can hide behind the noise of larger companies is a fatal fallacy.[66]

Colonial Pipeline paid a nearly $5 million ransom to get its data back. Hackers will squeeze every penny out of the ransom that they can. They often hang out in your systems when you're breached and have a good idea of what's in your bank account. Let's say they stole a record with 1,000 emails, and they know you have $100,000 in your bank account. They make the ransom $150,000 because they know your margin and are betting you can find a way to get additional funds. So, now you must decide whether to get a loan or say, "Screw you, I won't pay," and lose all your customer data to the dark web. The choice is yours.

However, a ransom is just the tip of the financial iceberg you're careening toward if you're noncompliant. After an attack, you're responsible for paying for the following:

- Repairing any damages due to the attack, like a monitoring service to find the leaked data online to try to make good with your customers (and that's *very* expensive)
- Staff wages to handle the influx of customer calls and emails in response to the breach
- Offering free or discounted products or services to customers to try to retain loyalty
- Hiring lawyers
- Hiring IT consultants or staff to fix the problem
- Hiring accountants or paying additional fees to existing accountants
- Hiring PR consultants to keep the breach quiet and maintain your reputation

Additionally, if you are found to be noncompliant after a cyberattack, you can forget about cyber insurance covering it. This can leave your organization financially exposed, bearing the full brunt of the costs associated with data breaches, ransomware attacks, or other cyberthreats.

According to a 2020 National Cybersecurity Alliance report, 60% of small companies that suffer a data breach go out of business within six months because they don't have the resources to bounce back from the financial costs.[67]

Damage to Your Reputation

Every state in the US and the District of Columbia, Puerto Rico, and the Virgin Islands has passed legislation requiring notification of a breach involving personal information.[68] Depending on the type of breach, there may also be industry requirements for notification. You can't pay a ransom and have the problem disappear. (You can try like Uber did in 2018, but it backfired. They looked terrible, not to mention they had to pay $148 million to settle claims over the cover-up.)[69]

When your clients or customers receive that message from you, will they say, "Oh, no worries!"? They'll likely say, "I'm really annoyed." It's not a given that they will walk away, but it doesn't make their decision to stay with you easy.

Big companies like Cash App and AT&T (both breached in 2022, with millions of people impacted) have the resources to withstand a tarnished reputation. But rebuilding trust and restoring reputation is challenging for small and midsize businesses with more limited resources. If you lose your customer's confidential data, they can find someone else who doesn't have that bruise on their reputation. Customers are increasingly concerned about the security of their personal information and are quick to sever ties with businesses that fail to protect their data. According to Thales's survey of more than 10,000 consumers around the globe, 70% would stop doing business with companies after a data breach.[70] Your reputation is priceless.

Legal Liabilities

Data protection and privacy regulations hold businesses accountable for safeguarding customer data in the United States. For example, HIPAA applies to health care organizations, while the Gramm-Leach-Bliley Act covers financial institutions. Failing to meet these compliance requirements can result in severe penalties and legal action from regulatory bodies such as the Federal Trade Commission and the Office for Civil Rights. Colonial Pipeline still faces a $1 million fine from the Department of Transportation's Pipeline and Hazardous Materials Safety Administration for not providing adequate documents to demonstrate compliance.[71]

Customers are prepared to hold you accountable for noncompliance too. This happened to Allscripts, a Chicago-based medical record software company, in 2018 when hackers attacked it using malware to block its clients from patient files. Instead of paying a ransom, Allscripts restored access via a secure backup. Still, it took a week for the company to fix the problem and give their nearly 1,500 affected clients access to their patient records. One of Allscripts' clients, however, sued the software company for "significant business interruption and disruption and lost revenues"[72] due to Allscripts "failing to take adequate and reasonable measures to implement, monitor, and audit its data systems, which could have prevented [the breach]."[73] Allscripts faces a class action lawsuit and all the financial and reputation damage that goes along with it.

Decreased Employee Morale

We're learning that a long-lasting consequence of cyberattacks and noncompliance in businesses is employee morale. Imagine being responsible for protecting the company's sensitive data and IT infrastructure but not having the necessary resources or support to ensure its security. Noncompliance puts the company at risk and burdens IT teams heavily, causing stress and job dissatisfaction.

It's not just IT staff. According to a study by Encore, more than half of *all* employees in an organization would have second thoughts about belonging to a company that recently suffered a data breach. After an attack, employees doubt a company's ethics, values, and responsibility to customers and employees. On the other hand, when SMBs prioritize compliance and provide their employees with the necessary resources, training, and support, it not only boosts morale but also empowers them to make safer decisions and safeguard their company's assets effectively.

Time and Resources

Recovering from a data breach can be time-consuming and resource-intensive for small and medium-sized businesses. Companies may need to divert resources from other areas to address the breach. Fifty percent of SMBs report that it took more than twenty-four hours to recover from an attack, and 25% said they lost business due to downtime.[74]

When Your Luck Runs Out, Compliance Is What Saves You

Compliance can be a bureaucratic nightmare. The red tape, paperwork, and audits make even the most resilient among us tear our hair out. We're entrepreneurs, innovators, and risk-takers; we thrive on agility and freedom. The idea of being bogged down by endless forms and regulations can feel suffocating, hindering our ability to adapt and grow. So, we resist compliance and instead write passwords down on index cards and sticky notes, don't implement employee security awareness training consistently (or at all), and refuse to put funds toward essential security tools.

However, regulators expect you to protect your data like you would your child. Do you leave the doors and windows open when you put your children to bed at night? Do you lock your doors? Do you have a gate around your house or a guard dog? How many different layers will a burglar have to pass through to get into your home? Does the risk outweigh the temporary cost savings? This is how you must think when it comes to the data that's in your possession.

Compliance doesn't mean you need to replace your whole IT infrastructure. An MSP or MSSP can implement a few simple tweaks and offer 24/7 management and oversight, dramatically decreasing your risk and significantly reducing the cost of a breach. Compliance is an investment in your future, protecting your businesses from costly breaches and maintaining the trust of your customers. When your luck runs out and hackers find your weakness, noncompliance devastates your business.

Compliance is what saves it.

About Cora

Cora Park understands what it's like to sit across the table as a small business owner, knowing your success lies in trusting that the advice you're given is accurate and has your best interests in mind. She also knows what it's like when that trust is mishandled and has devastating consequences.

During the '80s and '90s, Cora, along with her husband and business partner, Tom, ran a multimillion-dollar direct mail marketing company. By the time Cora was thirty-eight years old, with more than a decade of entrepreneurship experience, the pair had sold their successful printing and direct mail company and were looking forward to a fun passion project. They pitched the investment opportunity of opening two indoor dining and ice cream shop franchise locations—it was perfect.

Regrettably, adverse corporate guidance that didn't consider their ownership business needs resulted in enormous critical investment losses. Cora learned a valuable lesson about the importance of understanding businesses as individuals—not just as an extension of a corporate agenda. She didn't lament for long though and was hot on the heels of another opportunity as sales and marketing director with a local MSP entrepreneur. After several successful years at the MSP, Cora was asked if she'd be interested in buying the company. While she'd fallen in love with the MSP world, the business was another franchise and not an environment she wanted to return to as a business owner. At the same time, the IT industry was undergoing a massive shift.

HIPAA compliance regulators were coming down on medical practices that were given a set date to meet stringent compliance rules. This resulted in significant changes to how medical practices of all varieties managed, stored, and shared patient data. The dangers of not protecting data were coming to the surface, and the forewarnings of the future cybersecurity storm were brewing.

In 2013, Cora reentered the world of entrepreneurship—this time solo—and founded her MSP Diamond Business Communications (DBC, or Diamond for short), a cybersecurity-centric technology management company helping SMBs and nonprofits better serve their community by efficiently transforming their business workflows with proven processes, compliance safeguards, and reliable technology.

As president and CEO of DBC, Cora is fiercely committed to providing clients with the accurate and individualized attention they deserve and need to succeed.

With nearly every process and document living within digital and automated systems today and the increasing complexity of compliance regulations, Cora believes MSPs are as crucial to a business's success as its accountant or attorney. As an entrepreneur for over three decades, she understands the unique challenges cybersecurity compliance places on small and midsize businesses. She seeks to make compliance as simple and stress-free as possible for her clients.

When Cora isn't conquering the compliance world, she takes her passion for fitness and philanthropy to the trail. She enjoys the challenge of an occasional triathlon, like the New Jersey State Triathlon, and supporting charitable 3K and 5K events. She's a travel and beach enthusiast and enjoys culinary dining adventures with her beloved husband, family, and close friends.

For more information, contact Cora at Diamond Business Communications:

Email: Cora@Diamondbc.net
Phone: (609) 642-9300
Web: www.Diamondbc.net
LinkedIn: www.linkedin.com/in/corapark

Chapter 17

THE COST OF NONCOMPLIANCE IS THE VALUE OF YOUR BUSINESS AND— BOTTOM LINE—YOUR REVENUES

Duane Lansdowne

D id you know that just a single breach can destroy the value of your business entirely? Did you know a breach could even threaten the assets of a business's owners and executives?

This can happen if authorities find out you're noncompliant with regulations after a breach.

Imagine if you had to face an angry client who sued you because you didn't perform your due diligence in protecting their data. Could you face the reputational loss that results from going through court?

Would your business survive if you had to pay the client compensation?

If you want to convince management that you need to meet compliance regulations despite the costs, you must show them the financial costs of getting breached and caught while noncompliant.

I know it can be a hard sell. Company owners want to make as much profit as possible, and compliance can seem like a huge roadblock. I know many stories where business operations and IT have butted heads over this issue.

So, here's how you can make the case to them that compliance protects the ability of your business to generate profit. By the time you're done reading this chapter, you'll have solid arguments to offer if management tries to push back on the costs of compliance. You can give executives a clear understanding of the importance of cybersecurity and compliance in an increasingly technology-driven world.

Let's Count the Costs

Getting breached is bad, no question about it. It can set your business on fire. However, getting breached while noncompliant is like pouring gasoline on a fire. If you're in an industry with heavy regulations, you can also toss in a few sticks of dynamite.

What's burning up? Your revenues and your reputation. Staying noncompliant puts these at risk. Here's how.

State and Federal Fines

State and federal agencies enforce regulatory requirements on businesses to protect customers and clients. Different industries must follow different regulatory requirements. For example:

- Patients want to know you're protecting their health information.
- Anyone using a credit card wants confidence that their information will stay between them and the merchant.
- Governments want to know their secrets are secure the way Controlled Unclassified Information (CUI) is protected.

When a company is caught breaking regulations, state and federal regulators can levy huge fines and require changes to business operations:

- A violation of HIPAA can cost from $25,000 to $1.5 million for all violations of a single requirement in a calendar year.
- Violations of the Federal Trade Commission's Children's Online Privacy Protection Act (COPPA) can bring penalties of up to $40,000 per violation per day.
- Gramm-Leach-Bliley Act violations can force your company to pay penalties of up to $1 million per day, plus many other financial penalties to restore money to affected parties, including reforming contracts and return of assets.
- CMMC violations can not only get you fined but block your company from further government contracts.

- Noncompliance with General Data Protection Regulation has cost companies millions of dollars for privacy breaches.

Sadly, enough executives have ignored compliance regulations so that some regulatory laws now require third-party independent auditing to confirm compliance. If you're audited and found wanting, you'll be in the crosshairs of government attention.

You might think you're too small to get noticed by regulators, but it takes just one whistleblower, one breach, or one required audit to expose you.

Should your business survive the penalties, you can also bet that the regulators will force you to take action to become compliant on their timetable, not yours.

It is alarming to note that cyberattacks have significant consequences for small businesses. According to a 2018 Inc.com article, a staggering 60% of small businesses are forced to close their doors within just six months of falling victim to a cyberattack. This highlights the critical importance of having a robust cybersecurity strategy in place, no matter your business size.

What is even more concerning is that a substantial 62% of 1,377 C-level executives of small businesses surveyed admitted that their firms do not have an up-to-date or active cybersecurity strategy or technology in place. Some even reported having no strategy at all.

While some basic measures, like antivirus programs, might be in place on individual computers, a comprehensive assessment of risks and proactive steps to address network security vulnerabilities is often missing. The reality is that many C-level executives may not fully grasp the potential consequences on their business of a data breach or noncompliance.

A breach can cause devastating financial losses, reputational damage, and loss of customer trust. It is crucial for small businesses to understand that cybersecurity is not just an option but a necessity in today's digital landscape. The relentless warnings from news outlets and the technology community aim to raise awareness about the ever-increasing cybersecurity threats businesses face.

By proactively addressing cybersecurity risks and staying up-to-date with the latest security measures, small businesses can safeguard their operations, protect their customers' data, and ensure their longevity in an increasingly interconnected world.

Investing in a well-rounded cybersecurity strategy, which includes regular risk assessments, employee training, network monitoring, and incident response planning, can significantly reduce a company's chances of falling victim to cyberattacks.

So, management has a choice: spend money now and get all the benefits of compliance and protection from fines, or spend the same money on a faster schedule and get fined on top of it.

And that's just the first cost of noncompliance.

Lawsuits and Settlements

If your clients discover that someone stole their information or money from you, you could face a lawsuit. If you weren't compliant, expect to lose. Data privacy lawsuits are a genuine threat.

National companies have faced these lawsuits after breaches and lost badly. Amazon, Equifax, Home Depot, Capital One, Uber, Morgan Stanley, and Yahoo! have all settled lawsuits against them to the tune of tens or hundreds of millions of dollars.

Sometimes, it's not even data loss you're being sued for. It's theft of money. Here's one example where a hacker stole money after a breach.

A nonprofit organization was working with a general contractor to build a new facility. They were negotiating by email and came to an agreement on the project and how to pay for it.

A hacker had been watching the emails go back and forth for some time. When the moment came for the nonprofit to send the money to the contractor, the hacker got the money—hundreds of thousands of dollars—sent to them.

Neither the nonprofit nor the contractor knew someone was watching the conversation, but both lost out. The nonprofit lost their money, and the contractor also experienced losses.

It's quite possible that one side could blame the other for letting the hacker breach their systems and seek restitution in a lawsuit. But even if you win a lawsuit, you still have to pay for lawyers, and defendants always pay more.

Loss of Reputation and Credibility

Let's say you have the money to pay the fines and stand up to the lawsuits. Even if you survive those costs, what will your customers and clients think about your business after that?

A breach will damage your reputation, but you could explain it away if you can prove you were compliant. Sometimes, an attacker just gets lucky and finds a way in.

But if someone breached you because you were noncompliant and they found a gaping security hole? Say goodbye to your reputation!

You might also say goodbye to your market share. Your competition will tout their compliance certifications to lure your customer base away.

By the time you clean up after the breach and get compliant, the damage may be too great for you to stay in business.

The only way to minimize reputational hits after a breach is to have a solid plan for what to do after a breach. You'll have that plan if you follow compliance regulations. You'll have procedures in place on how to notify clients and restore business operations as soon as possible following a breach.

Loss of Business Momentum

Getting breached is like stumbling during a race. Just as it takes time to pick yourself up and keep going in a race, it will take time to seal the breach and repair the damage. This creates a drag on revenue, and it could take a long time to get back to where you were.

It will take much longer if you don't meet compliance standards. Most regulations require businesses to have secure backup and disaster recovery plans and to report if there was a data breach. These can be vital if you lose access to your data after a breach.

One of our clients, with 1,400 employees and several remote locations, got hit with ransomware that spread through the network. It took them three to four weeks to return to business again, and they had to start over with old data.

The cost of just getting back up and running was $50,000, plus the cost of new equipment and data forensics. You can bet that if you're noncompliant and have poor data recovery practices, the cost could be much more.

Exposure of Your Business Secrets

A breach could expose your trade secrets and other intellectual property, which could put you at a competitive disadvantage, but it takes time for hackers to find what they're looking for. In companies with strong compliance policies and cybersecurity, someone might get in and get detected within a couple of minutes. Cybersecurity would eject the attacker and then analyze how they got in to seal the hole.

The time between a breach and detection of the breach is called "dwell time." A cybersecurity goal is to make this as short as possible. The longer an attacker can work without detection, the more damage they can do.

A skilled hacker in the network of a business that's lazy about compliance could stay there for literal *months*, analyzing what's happening on that network, looking through files, and learning all they can about the company's secrets. How much is your company's intellectual property worth?

Companies with strong compliance have far shorter dwell times. If someone gets in, your team will have the tools and procedures to kick out the intruder quickly. Do it fast enough and a breach could paradoxically show that your company is on the ball!

Insurance Problems

More costs? You bet! Here's a new one that some businesses are discovering.

There are companies out there that decide that compliance is too expensive. Instead of paying for compliance, they rely on cyber insurance to cover the costs of breaches.

But insurance companies are famously averse to paying out. This trick will not work, if it ever did. Insurers require companies to state whether they comply with data protection regulations. If you get breached and the insurer finds out you lied about being compliant, they won't pay.

Some insurers get lied to enough that they're requiring third-party audits before approving a policy.

If you're paying for cyber liability, but you're not meeting the promises you've made to your insurance carrier, you're pouring your money down the drain.

You might as well not even have that policy. It's burning money.

You Are a Target No Matter the Size of Your Business

Take a moment to add up all those costs. Compare that number to any estimate you have for getting your company compliant. It's a near certainty that the costs of noncompliance are far greater.

Yet there is another argument we see a lot: "I'm too small to get noticed."

Major companies that get breached make the headlines, but did you know that criminals aim nearly half of all cyberattacks at small businesses?

Small businesses are often easy opportunities for cybercriminals because they're less likely to comply with regulations.

Also, small businesses can be a steppingstone to breaching larger businesses. If you have any clients with significant assets or intellectual property and you communicate even over something as simple as email, your small network could be used to gain access to your clients. Acquisitions and mergers present a perfect opportunity for a hacker to gain access to larger, more protected companies' networks because of the lack of cybersecurity among small businesses.

A related argument is that you're too small to be required to comply. This is incorrect. Nearly every company in the country, even a sole proprietorship, has some cybersecurity regulations they must follow.

A common national one is PCI DSS, which regulates the use of credit card information. If you accept payment by credit card, you must comply with PCI DSS. Yes, even if you're a sole proprietor!

Protect Your Revenue by Becoming Compliant

Cybersecurity and regulations protect data, but that's just a means to an end—protecting your company's ability to generate revenue. That's the crucial piece of information that executives need to understand.

Paying for compliance may be expensive in the short term, but it will protect your business down the road. The costs we've mentioned can easily exceed the value of your business if you're breached, noncompliant, and not protected from cyberattacks.

Noncompliance isn't a technical problem. It's a financial problem. Operating your business while ignoring compliance and cybersecurity puts your business at risk of failure. You could even find yourself legally liable for a lack of diligence if you're breached.

How's that for convincing management they have a fiduciary responsibility to become compliant with data protection regulations?

How Do I Become Compliant?

If your C-suite is unwilling to pay for compliance, share with them the information you've just learned. The costs of noncompliance are far greater than they know. After you get buy-in, the next step is to get your business audited by a competent MSP that has a strong cybersecurity focus.

Some things to look for are Certified CMMC Professionals on staff and a managed security services provider service that knows your industry's regulations. MSPs on staff can create credible preparation and action plans to help you get compliant before you get audited or to assist in representing or preparing an organization for formal assessment.

One word of warning. Don't trust a security vendor that relies only on software as their compliance product. It's true that having the right software is critical to managing your compliance, mapping out your activities to prove you are doing what you say to protect your business. But real security and compliance must involve the entire business, from management to HR to your IT department. It entails a lot of documentation and ongoing verification.

Once your business is compliant, you'll be ready for nearly everything an attacker or a regulator could throw at you. You won't have to worry about paying far more than you need to if you ever get breached, and you may just save your business from collapse.

Lastly, keep in mind that regulators could audit organization compliance at any time! Are you ready?

About Duane

Duane Lansdowne is the president and owner of Acclamar Financial & Technology Consulting Group. He founded his firm in Arlington, Virginia, in 2010 to help clients run their businesses by the numbers and to leverage technology to help them grow in a competitive market, protected in a world of cybercriminals.

Duane's entire life has been devoted to the passionate pursuit of helping others. Currently, he helps business owners align their challenges with their objectives to achieve their goals through professional management and advisory consulting services.

Prior to entering the information technology industry, Duane worked as an emergency medical technician and a firefighter, for which he received the Firefighter Rookie of the Year Award from the department in 1995. He continued his training from confined space and trench rescue to structural collapse and vehicle extrication. During this time, he also worked at a hospital for over eight years, providing ambulatory patient care.

After a serious car accident, Duane went back to college in 2002 to pursue a degree in computer information science in information technology/networking. That led to his full-time jump into IT when he worked for an IT consulting firm. He expanded his knowledge and experience as a network engineer and IT consultant, providing solutions for small to medium-sized businesses, including local and federal government.

Duane helped design the first video conferencing manual for the US Department of Health and Human Services, providing implementation and training to allow the department to conduct meetings over video conferencing to cut down on travel costs.

Following his tenure at the IT consulting firm, he became the information technology manager for the City of Manassas Park local government. He was responsible for individual departments and over 150 employees, ensuring the full functionality of six city buildings—including the town's police/E911, social services, and fire departments—with regulatory compliance, information technology security, and IT support requirements.

Over the course of his career, Duane developed a love for educating customers about the importance of security and compliance in these heavily regulated fields.

He founded Acclamar as a consulting, financial, and MSP firm to help businesses understand that they need to lean into compliance and prevent cyberattacks so they can become competitive in a technology-driven world and cultivate growth in their industry.

Acclamar specializes in helping health care organizations, medical practices, law firms, local governments, local and federal contractors, construction companies, and other small businesses with their IT, cybersecurity, and compliance needs.

Acclamar's focus is helping businesses prevent problems, not fixing them after the fact. Compliance with data privacy and cybersecurity regulations is a major component of this mission.

For more information, contact Duane at Acclamar:

Email: duane@acclamar.com
Phone: (703) 270-1007
Web: www.acclamar.com
LinkedIn: www.linkedin.com/in/duanelansdowneacclamar/

Chapter 18

THE GOVERNMENT DOESN'T CARE THAT YOU DIDN'T KNOW: HOW TO PROTECT YOURSELF FROM PAYING FINES AND GOING TO JAIL IF YOU GET HACKED

Christopher Brown

"Willful blindness."

It describes a situation where someone intentionally keeps themselves unaware of the facts to avoid civil or criminal liability. Whether your "blindness" is intentional or unintentional, it's not a valid defense to avoid fines, penalties, or jail time. Regulatory bodies and enforcement agencies expect organizations to be aware of (and comply with) all laws, regulations, and standards pertaining to their industry. And here's the thing: Claiming willful blindness can work against you should you be hacked or found to be noncompliant. It could be viewed as being negligent, and your organization may be seen as not taking responsibility for your compliance commitments seriously.

If company management is risking jail time, their company being fined, reputation loss, and so on, why aren't all companies in the United States compliant? There are a few reasons. On top of willful (or intentional) blindness, the complexity and ever-changing nature of compliance can be daunting. Also, achieving and maintaining compliance may require investments in technology, training, personnel, and other resources—an investment that might lose out to other company priorities that are higher on the list. Plus, in my experience, I've found that people often assume that being hacked is something that happens to somebody else. Some businesspeople view compliance as hindering their daily and future business goals. They know enforcement agencies are not proactively contacting companies and asking them to verify that their business is compliant. They may even feel that if they're caught, whatever fine is levied will be less than the costs associated with compliance.

That said, many organizations do prioritize compliance. They understand that compliance is about maintaining trust with their customers and vendors, ensuring the security and privacy of the data they've been entrusted with, and protecting their hard-earned reputation. They are painfully aware that hackers are becoming increasingly sophisticated, and they must take the proper precautions to thwart them at every turn. If you are one of the companies that prioritizes compliance (or want to be), consider this your checklist for what you should be doing today to avoid being fined (or experiencing jail time) should you get hacked.

- **Leadership.** Great leaders inspire and motivate their employees. They set the vision for their company and outline its purpose, values, and objectives. They make important decisions and are excellent at solving problems. As a leader, you must be a positive influence and demonstrate a strong commitment to compliance. You must keep yourself informed about the cybersecurity threats that could put your company at risk. You must communicate the importance of compliance, then set a plan in motion and hold people accountable to implement it.

- **Compliance education.** As the saying goes, the chain is only as strong as its weakest link. It only takes one employee to click one link in a fraudulent email for your business to become a victim of a cyberattack. Your employees must be trained on hackers' methods to infiltrate computers, such as phishing emails or malicious websites. They need to understand their responsibilities regarding compliance and the ramifications for the company if best practices are not followed.

- **Policies and procedures.** Comprehensive policies and procedures must be developed (and regularly updated) that outline your company's expectations regarding compliance. They should be easily accessible to all employees.

- **Communication.** All employees must feel comfortable reporting any compliance concerns or violations. Implement anonymous reporting mechanisms, such as a confidential email or hotline, that employees can use to report violations without fear of retaliation. Plus, reinforce the importance of compliance in your newsletter and at team meetings.

- **Accountability and enforcement.** If someone does violate compliance protocols, hold them accountable. Also, reward and/or acknowledge employees who consistently demonstrate a commitment to compliance.
- **Keep all your software up-to-date.** Ensure all your devices are running the latest operating system updates, virus protection software, firewalls, browsers, plug-ins, security patches, and intrusion detection systems. Outdated versions often have vulnerabilities that hackers love to exploit for gain.
- **Use two-factor authentication.** Employees who log in to your website or application should use two-factor authentication. Two-factor authentication requires a second form of identification (a code sent to their phone, a code generated by a 2FA application, smart cards, facial or fingerprint recognition, etc.). This adds another layer of security that helps to ensure that only authorized people will have access to your data and accounts.
- **Back up your data.** According to the 2019 *World Backup Day Survey* results, 97% of businesses back up their data at least once a year, and 86% perform backups monthly, weekly, and daily. This still leaves 14% who either don't back up their data or only back up "at least once a year." The same survey found that 29% of businesses suffered a data loss that led to downtime. You should never rely on one source to store important information. A copy of your data should be stored in a cloud or on one or more external hard drives. At the very least, print out and keep essential documents in a safe place.
- **Use strong passwords.** You must make it mandatory that your employees always use strong passwords (at least eight characters long, containing a combination of uppercase and lowercase letters, numbers, and special characters such as !, #, %, or $). Additionally, change your passwords every three months and never use the same password for multiple accounts.
- **Familiarize yourself with state and federal regulations.** Compliance regulations vary across different industries and areas of governance. In the United States, numerous federal regulations apply nationwide. Plus, many states have their own specific compliance regulations that complement and expand upon federal regulations. For example, in New York State, they have

what's called the New York State SHIELD Act. Their website discusses your obligations, the safeguards you are expected to take to prevent a breach, and who to contact if a breach occurs. They also discuss the penalties for companies that violate the SHIELD Act: *"Under the SHIELD Act, the Attorney General may seek injunctive relief, restitution, and penalties against any business entity for violating the law. For failure to provide timely notification, the court may impose a civil penalty of up to $20 per instance of failed notification, not to exceed $250,000. For failure to maintain reasonable safeguards, the court may impose a civil penalty of up to $5,000 per violation."* Search online for your federal and state compliance information.

- **Monitor your bank accounts.** Regularly review the activity of bank accounts, credit cards, or other financial tools for suspicious or unusual activity. If something is amiss, contact your provider immediately.

- **Develop an incident response plan.** An incident response plan for compliance is a documented framework that outlines the processes, procedures, and actions to be taken in response to a security incident or breach to ensure compliance with applicable laws, regulations, and industry standards. Your incident response plan should include your objectives, the roles and responsibilities of everyone involved, and the methodology for identifying and reporting incidents. It should outline the incident response process (initial response, investigation and assessment, mitigation and recovery, communication and reporting) and the escalation procedures. This plan should be tested, evaluated, updated, and reviewed regularly.

- **Audits and monitoring.** It's essential to conduct regular audits and assessments to determine the compliance program's effectiveness, identify areas of noncompliance, and, if necessary, implement corrective actions.

- **Focus on remote users.** According to the US Census Bureau, in 2019, around nine million people worked from home. In 2021, the September 2022 *American Community Survey* found that the number had risen to 27.6 million. Are remote workers using their personal computers for work? If so, what type of security protections do they have? (The adage "Never mix business with pleasure" also applies to computers.) Are they accessing your network from coffee shops? Are they aware and wary of spoofed hotspots (evil twin Wi-Fi networks)? If they do financial transactions, are they all done over secured websites? These are just a few of the questions you need to ask.

- **Purchase cybersecurity insurance.** If you don't have cybersecurity insurance, consider buying coverage to help mitigate the financial impact of a cyberattack. Cybersecurity can cover you for the expenses related to the investigation, legal fees, customer notification, credit monitoring services, public relations, business interruption, and potential legal settlements/judgments.

- **Partner with a managed services provider.** An MSP possesses deep knowledge and expertise in regulatory requirements and best practices. They can also be very cost-effective at assembling and maintaining an in-house compliance team, which can be very resource-intensive, especially for small to medium-sized businesses. An MSP can tailor their services to meet your organization's unique compliance needs and demands. MSPs often have access to advanced security tools that may be too costly for a business to justify buying. Plus, when you partner with an MSP, it lets you focus on your core business with the peace of mind of knowing that all your compliance requirements are being taken care of.

The above are all actions you can take to increase the odds that you won't be hacked, and if you are hacked, you can demonstrate that you were taking compliance seriously, which will lessen the chances of you facing a harsh penalty. If you are hacked, here are some steps you can take to protect yourself from the legal and regulatory consequences:

- **Preserve evidence.** Take screenshots, save emails, and document any other relevant information related to the breach. Keep all evidence (emails, logs, etc.) that could identify the culprits and establish that you have taken compliance seriously.

- **Contact and fully cooperate with law enforcement.** Report the breach to your local law enforcement agency and cybercrime unit as soon as possible. Be prepared to provide them with evidence of the hack, such as logs and suspicious emails. Your cooperation and willingness to resolve the situation will work in your favor if you later face a fine or penalty. Check the section of your state's website that deals with cybersecurity for whom it instructs you to contact.

- **Seek legal advice.** Contact an attorney specializing in cybercrime or digital law. They will help you understand your legal rights and obligations and the best action to take moving forward.
- **Strengthen your security.** To protect yourself against another (or future) attack, change all passwords, enable two-factor authentication, update your software and devices, and install reliable security solutions.
- **Document your remedial actions.** Document all the steps (removing malware, updating security measures, implementing new safeguards, etc.) you've taken to mitigate the hack's impact. Doing so shows your commitment to resolving the situation and preventing future breaches.
- **Partner with an MSP.** Now is the time to do so if you haven't partnered with a managed services provider yet. An MSP will assist you in data recovery and getting your systems back online and operating. Plus, they will put a plan together to get your business compliant as soon as possible.

By taking these steps, you can help protect your business from fines and legal liabilities in the event of a cyberattack. Remember that promoting a culture of compliance is an ongoing effort that requires commitment from all levels of your organization. It's essential to create an environment where employees understand the importance of compliance and feel supported in their compliance efforts.

About Chris

Chris Brown is the founder and CEO of Twin Networks, which serves the New England area. Twin Networks specializes in helping small to medium-sized businesses in financial, legal, architectural, and medical sectors meet all their IT, cybersecurity, and compliance requirements.

Chris has over twenty years of experience in the industry. In 2001, he worked as a network engineer for the law firm Robinson+Cole. In 2005, the University of Connecticut hired him as a network architect in their health center, where he worked for six years. Because the university dealt with a variety of systems and network architectures, Chris was exposed to a wide array of compliance requirements. In 2006, he founded Twin Networks, working part-time at night and on weekends. In 2011, the demand for Twin Networks' services exploded to the point where it required all of Chris's attention, so he left UConn Health to focus on Twin Networks full-time.

From a very early age, Chris was instilled with a lifelong passion for learning. Technology became his ideal focus because it continuously reinvents itself at a breakneck pace. Because of the rapidly changing nature of technology, know-how, and compliance regulations, Chris recognized that smaller businesses need assistance as they are required to meet the same regulatory requirements as larger businesses.

As someone who views small business owners as the backbone of America, Chris focuses on helping them meet all their cybersecurity and compliance requirements. His goal is to help small businesses—many of whom, through no fault of their own, are using outdated hardware and software—upgrade their technology to make them more productive and save them money over the long term. He views Twin Networks' role as a trusted advisor and partner, helping his clients optimize the efficiency of their business through technology, allowing them to focus on their primary business of selling their products and services.

For Chris, integrity is paramount. He prides himself that he and the Twin Networks team hold themselves to the highest ethical standards. They demand excellence from themselves and everyone they associate with and only offer their clients the highest quality products and services. They are always respectful to their clients, partners, competitors, and employees, and once they make a promise, they keep it.

In addition to compliance, Twin Networks' services include virtual chief information officer consulting, network security, data backup, disaster recovery, and managed IT. Plus, they offer Twin Cloud Backup, which protects their clients' vital systems and data and offers them the peace of mind of knowing their business and information are protected.

For more information, contact Chris at Twin Networks:

Email: cbrown@twinnetworks.com
Phone: (860) 399-1244
Web: www.twinnetworks.com

Chapter 19

HOW MUCH COMPLIANCE
IS RIGHT FOR YOU?
Robert Sparre

O *r perhaps the better question is, how fast are you willing to run from a charging bear?*

There is a simple strategy to outrunning a grizzly bear. The key is not to be faster than the bear; you just need to be faster than your friends.

While this method doesn't guarantee your safety, it certainly increases the odds of your survival. Like most apex predators, bears will almost always choose to conserve energy by going for the easier meal: the crippled elk, the low-hanging mulberry, the salmon or . . . the slowest among your friends. Sure, a grizzly *could* attack a moose bull, but the risk of injury and failure is much, much higher. Instead, they'll wade patiently in a rushing stream until a salmon plops right between their jaws.

Like a grizzly, cybercriminals will prey on low-hanging fruit first—the easy targets. What makes a target easy for a cyber attacker? A business that's not taking basic precautions to protect itself. The one cruising right along until they unexpectedly trip into a cyber attacker's trap. Many businesses fail to adequately defend themselves because, unlike a hunting bear, cyberthreats are largely invisible.

Only 34% of small businesses have a cybersecurity plan in place, according to the *CNBC/SurveyMonkey Small Business Index*,[75] which means more than half of small businesses are moving at a snail's pace in front of the charging bear. They don't see, hear, or feel the danger breathing down their neck and don't know where to begin protecting themselves from seemingly invisible threats.

A good way to think about cybercrime is that it's like car theft. Cybercriminals operate the same way as car thieves. They walk down a quiet street, flipping car door handles to see if they're locked. They aren't going to start bashing windows open right away. That would draw a lot of unwanted attention and ruin their chances of making off with the stolen cash and AirPods. What they do is creep past all the locked handles until they find one that gives way and then—jackpot. This is a criminal activity we can see, and the protections—clicking the lock button on your key every time you leave your car until it beeps back a confirmation that it's secure—are things we can see and hear too.

Cybercriminals work with methods similar to those of car thieves, but they're not as easy to see and hear—*unless* you know what you're looking for.

That's precisely what compliance is about. Compliance is your tangible strategy, implementation, and follow-through of a robust cybersecurity infrastructure with all the locks, bells, whistles, and alarms. By embracing compliance, you become the bull moose, not the salmon.

Compliance vs. Security

One of the best ways to put greater space between you and the bear is to embrace compliance, not just security—because there's a difference between the two.

- *Security* involves the specific systems, software, policies, and controls you put in place to protect your company's physical and intellectual assets.
- *Compliance* typically refers to meeting security requirements put in place by third-party regulatory agencies as part of a carefully designed framework of recommendations. In many industries, meeting compliance standards is *not* optional. If you fail to meet them, you will be hammered by insurance claim denials, regulatory fines, and much higher costs after an attack.

Another way to compare security and compliance is "should do" vs. "have to do." In nearly all cases, the things you MUST do to be compliant are the same things you SHOULD do to protect yourself anyway. The primary difference is that compliance requires additional documentation, and if you're breached, you will be audited and evaluated for your ability to meet compliance standards. If the audit reveals you didn't meet compliance standards, you'll have bigger problems than a breach.

Why Compliance Is Nonnegotiable

I often hear from clients that the kind of data they have is not data cybercriminals care enough about to steal and sell on the black market. Twenty years ago, that might have been the case. In the '90s and early 2000s, cybercrime and ransomware attacks primarily targeted large companies, like hospitals and government organizations, who were forced to pay millions of dollars in ransom costs.

Today, the landscape is drastically different. You might be thinking that no one cares about your data. Maybe you have credit card numbers, Social Security numbers, addresses, or other personal information about your customers. You're probably right: only you (and maybe your customer) really need or care about your data.

But cybercriminals know that *you* care about your data. They know you need it to run your business. They know that if you lose it, a lot is at stake, like your reputation, customer loyalty, and maybe even your livelihood. They believe you will pay handsomely to get it back. Often, they're right. Forty-five percent of businesses attacked by ransomware paid the ransom, according to a report by Coveware.[76]

Small businesses—even those with only twenty-five or fifty employees—are the prime prey because they don't have the knowledge, skills, or resources to protect themselves from attacks. Unprotected SMBs are the low-hanging fruit, the flailing salmon.

Still not sure if you're the lowest-hanging fruit on the mulberry tree? Let's find out. Here are a few questions to ask about your business:

1. Do you have cyber insurance? If so, are you meeting the conditions of your cyber insurance policy?
2. How long can you survive without access to your data or network systems before it negatively impacts your business?
3. How long would recovering and restoring business operations after an attack take?
4. How long could you continue to pay your staff during downtime?
5. How would you explain a breach to your employees? Your customers?
6. If you were the victim of a cyberattack, could you recover?

How many of these questions could you answer confidently? Do you feel good about your answers? If so, you're probably jogging far away from the bear at a steady pace. Great—keep going.

If you answered with any doubts, you might be lagging. Next, I'll walk you through how to get—and stay—ahead of the bear . . . er, the cybercriminals.

Taking One Step Is Way Better than Taking Zero

The problem that most companies are wading through isn't deciding how much compliance is right for them. The problem is that they don't have basic security in place to meet compliance requirements *at all*. Either because they don't take security and compliance seriously or they don't know where to start. Thankfully, the solution isn't complicated.

Just start with step one.

Taking a single step toward compliance can put you ahead of the bear. Doing SOMETHING to protect yourself is better than doing nothing. You don't have to fix everything in one day but get started. Chip away at it. Improve your security posture and compliance one bite at a time. By taking even some basic precautions, you'll begin to put more space between you and the bear.

The good news is that many compliance regulations overlap; they all start with the same basic standards. Start with these, and you go from walking to jogging away from the bear.

Secure Your Passwords and Accounts

One of the easiest ways hackers can get into your accounts is by cracking simple passwords. Add some complexity to your security by strengthening your account policies.

- A good password policy is a great place to start. Length is more important than complexity. In other words, a ten-character password is much better than eight characters. Even short passwords with complicated symbols are easier to crack than a longer, ten-character password. (I recommend going long, using at least twelve to sixteen characters, and do NOT reuse passwords across different systems!)
- Use a password manager! Please don't save passwords in a browser. Instead, use a password manager that puts your private information into a cipher or code called encryption. This is miles better than using a Word document, Excel spreadsheet, or Sticky Notes to save passwords. These are easily accessible to hackers.
- Enforce multifactor authentication (MFA), also called two-factor authentication, wherever possible for your logins to applications like Microsoft 365, Gmail, or Facebook.

- Adopt the practice of least privilege. This means you do not give access or permission to an account unless it is needed. Do not allow regular users, including yourself, to be an administrator. Use separate accounts with elevated privileges to perform administrative tasks. (This goes for your IT department as well.) Each admin resource should have a different account for administrative work, which can be logged for audit purposes.

Secure Your Systems

This is the hardware side of compliance. This is how you create a digital fortress around your systems and check for any holes that a hacker could sneak into.

- Encrypt all your business's hard drives, especially laptops, which are vulnerable to theft.
- Have a device monitoring system (or outsource this to an MSP) for antivirus updates, security patches, etc. If you do this internally, make sure it gets checked daily.
- Run monthly network health checks, such as updating firmware in firewalls, switches, routers, and wireless access points.
- Have a good backup policy, especially air-gapped backups, to ensure survivability from a ransomware attack. Air-gapped backups store a copy of your data offline, so it's not accessible.
- Run security vulnerability scans once a quarter to alert you to new vulnerabilities or flaws in your system, network, hardware, or software.

Train Your Team

This is something many businesses are not used to doing but that will be on every compliance regulation list because your people are your biggest risk factor. Hackers prey on your employees through phishing emails, voicemail scams, and social engineering. Here's how to train a secure and compliant team:

- Conduct a security awareness training program for all employees and have regular follow-ups with existing staff.
- Don't make security exceptions for management, such as using non-expiring passwords or not enforcing MFA. Don't allow management to undermine

the culture of compliance. This will lead to failure and animosity among your staff, and you will have wasted your investment. I recently experienced an incident where a high-level partner was exempted from email filtering. A phishing email went into their inbox and caused a massive breach that cost them more than a week of downtime and required rebuilding their systems from scratch. Yeah, not good (not to mention embarrassing for that individual).

- Discuss security and compliance regularly with staff, even if it's just a brief encouraging message to stay the course on training. Tell them you appreciate the extra effort it takes to deal with the inconvenience, but remind them how critical it is to the business and their jobs to avoid a breach.
- Hire a compliance officer or engage with an MSP or MSSP to manage a compliance program that's right for you. Even if you outsource your compliance, you will need a designated liaison in your organization responsible for it.

But Which Compliance Regulations Are Relevant to My Business?

Generally, different industries and businesses will adhere to compliance regulations specific to their industry. Sometimes more than one. For example, medical practices will follow HIPAA and PHI guidelines. If they also handle credit card information, they'll follow PCI compliance. If they also have a cyber insurance policy, they'll have a separate set of standards outlined by the insurance provider. Many of the standards will overlap.

A fantastic place to start putting all the pieces together is with your managed services provider. Ask them if they have compliance programs in place or if they offer these services. You can also ask your cyber insurance carrier if they have any requirements.

Pro Tip: Ask your agent or broker if you can get any discounts on premiums by meeting certain conditions.

Another great place to look is your local industry association. For example, the industries listed below must adhere to one or more regulating bodies:

- Medical: HIPAA and PHI regulations
- Legal: American Bar Association and, in the EU, GDPR

- Finance: Sarbanes-Oxley
- Manufacturing: ITAR, PCI, GDPR, Sarbanes-Oxley
- Nonprofits: IRS and state tax forms, charitable solicitation licenses, conflict of interest, and clear governing bylaws

A simple way to learn more about compliance in your industry is to ask your peers. What are they following? What policies do they have in place?

Is All This Compliance Stuff Really Necessary?

No, you do not need to do any of this *unless* you're concerned about any of the following results of noncompliance:

- Increased susceptibility to cyberattacks.
- Severely damaging your reputation in your industry if/when you are breached.
- Unforgiving fines when personally identifiable information is stolen.
- Lower likelihood of getting cyber insurance.
- The bear sees you as the slowest runner and lowest-hanging fruit.

If you get started today and create a monthly meeting of at least one hour with your leadership and IT teams, you will be amazed at how much progress you can make! Ideally, host your meetings every two weeks in the beginning until you get into a rhythm. But don't do it less than once per month.

The Risks Are Real, but You're Not Alone

Working with an MSP or MSSP specializing in compliance can help you set up safeguards to keep you ahead of the pack. Doing even one thing and moving the needle toward improved compliance will put you miles ahead of SMBs stuck at step zero.

At a minimum, start with the following five steps:

1. Basic security software, such as antivirus and filtering software, that recognizes ransomware attack patterns.
2. Security updates to your operating system, often called "patches."
3. Application updates to all your software. Don't ignore these updates.

4. Air-gapped backups of your data.
5. Regular team training on cybersecurity best practices, like how to spot phishing emails and good password hygiene.

These things will keep you ahead of the slowest SMB, who refuses to believe the grizzly bear is chasing them. Oh, it is—and it's hungry. Cybercriminals are greedy and intelligent. They know your weaknesses, and they know what's important to you. When you set up protections and use basic security best practices outlined in compliance standards, you are putting more and more distance between you and relentless attackers.

What's step one for you today? Is it calling your MSP to make sure you are hitting all your compliance requirements? Is it checking in with your insurance policy to make sure you're making good on everything you need to? Or is it a quick call to your IT professional to make sure all your applications and systems are up-to-date?

Just pick one and go for it. If you're unsure where to start or don't have a compliance and security specialized MSP on your side, I'd be happy to help however I can.

About Robert

Robert Sparre, also known as "the guy who labels his label maker," is CEO of Dorset Connects, which he founded in September 1997. He didn't even know what a computer was until 1982 when he bought a Texas Instruments TI-99/4A for $49 at JC Penney.

Since then, he's written a book on Banyan VINES and SCO UNIX, as well as tons of detailed documentation on subjects ranging from building Linux boxes and Check Point firewalls to creating how-tos on wireless and VoIPs.

Today, Dorset Connects employs a team of over twenty, who together serve approximately seventy small to midsize businesses across the Greater Philadelphia region.

Robert believes their success boils down to their ability to handle ALL aspects of your IT infrastructure, including hardware and software management, vendor relationships, Internet connectivity, cloud hosting, and all other related technology needs.

Keeping your business secure can be overwhelming. It's not important for you to understand everything, but you do need to make sure your IT helper or outsourced IT managed services provider can do the job.

One factor that makes Dorset Connects unique is that they hire only seasoned, professional technicians whom they provide with continuing education opportunities on a regular basis to ensure they stay current with the latest technology. Dorset Connects' entire corporate culture is based on the book *The Ideal Team Player* by Patrick Lencioni, which emphasizes that your company should be "Hungry, Humble, and Smart."

- HUNGRY means always wanting to do more, always wanting to know more.
- HUMBLE stresses the importance of NOT hoarding information. There's a tendency for technical people to do this because they want to be "The Guy." No—you want to be *a team*.
- And SMART isn't about IQ; it's about EQ—emotional intelligence. We can teach someone technical information, but we want everyone to focus on social skills that can make a huge difference in customer service.

This "Hungry, Humble, and Smart" philosophy drives everything Dorset Connects does and has had a tremendous positive effect on the services they provide to customers as well as on employee morale.

Robert graduated from the University of Tampa in 1977 with a Bachelor of Music. He went on to get his associate degree in electronics from Delaware Technical Community College in 1986. His past careers include bowling alley mechanic, nursery and landscaping worker, musician, ice-cream truck driver, butcher, chef, network engineer, and consultant. In his spare time, he plays in a jazz band and makes rap videos about cybersecurity.

For more information, contact Robert at Dorset Connects:

Email: help@dorsetconnects.com
Phone: (484) 845-1600
Web: www.dorsetconnects.com

Chapter 20

HOW TO ENSURE YOU HAVE EXACTLY THE RIGHT COMPLIANCE STRATEGY WITHOUT OVERSPENDING—WHAT YOU DON'T KNOW REALLY CAN HURT YOU

Jeremy Valverde

There's no question that regulations have complicated the field of cybersecurity compliance. A business might have to comply with three or more different regulations, each with their own requirements.

Cost sensitivity is one reason a business may shy away from complying, but this is dangerous. If you get breached and are found to have been noncompliant, you could face fines that could destroy your business. Even if you can pay, you'll face reputational loss that will drive your clients to the competition.

Noncompliance with regulations can even destroy your chances of selling your company. We know of a company that went through an acquisition phase that fell through because of their lack of cybersecurity and regulatory compliance. The purchaser felt the risk to their business was too great. This was an immense blow to the company's valuation.

Noncompliance isn't an option, but, without the help of an expert, it's incredibly easy to overspend on compliance. Here's how you can ensure you have exactly the right compliance strategy without blowing your budget.

How Companies Overspend on Compliance

As cybercriminals continue to improve their art, the regulations on businesses keep getting tighter. Noncompliance exposes companies to risk from criminals and auditors. There are a lot of vendors offering solutions to compliance issues, but it's very easy to overspend on solutions.

Many of these software solutions may be excessive for your company's compliance needs and cause you to overspend. One example is a security information and event management (SIEM) tool. These tools provide real-time analysis of security alerts and logs generated by applications and network hardware. They can automatically implement security measures when they detect something is wrong.

In a huge enterprise network, these tools are vital in the fight against breaches because there are so many attack vectors. A team of humans cannot monitor everything on such an enormous network, so these tools are critical. The vendors of these tools know this and charge accordingly. For a small business with just four employees and a few computers, a SIEM is overkill.

If you want to spend less, you have to know the difference between security and compliance and have a strong compliance plan that will get your business in line with regulations without disrupting your business operations.

Security vs. Compliance

There is tension inside many businesses between operations and cybersecurity. Operations tries to push the business forward to get tasks done to generate profit, and security tries to stop operations from doing things that put the business at risk. This can create conflicts.

Compliance is the firewall between these two sides. A compliance strategy sets up boundaries for both sides. It tells operations how much security they need to prevent unwanted regulatory action, loss of profit, or loss of business valuation. It also tells cybersecurity teams how far they can go without compromising business operations.

When a company doesn't know how compliance fits in with business processes, it's easy to overspend on security. A security vendor might offer a suite of products that are too expensive or unnecessary for your business size or industry.

Worse, some vendors or companies rely too heavily on technology and think that's enough to keep them safe from regulators. Compliance strategy involves much more than having a few software packages. It also involves documentation, employee training, and more.

Therefore, if you need to comply with regulations, you need to have someone with experience in the compliance field to help you create the right strategy that covers your regulatory needs without overspending.

Five Steps to Finding the Right Compliance Strategy

At Affinity Tech Solutions, we use a five-step process to help businesses find the right compliance strategy while controlling costs.

1. Understand Which Regulations Apply

Even businesses with no computers still have regulations they must follow regarding personal identifiable information, but most businesses store PII and other protected data on computers. There are at least half a dozen different laws that require unique protections. The first step to compliance is understanding which of them apply to you.

Some of the major ones include:

- PCI DSS: for any business that uses, stores, or transmits credit card information
- GDPR: for any business that has customers in the European Union
- HIPAA: for all businesses that handle medical data
- CMMC: for businesses that have contracts with the government, particularly the Department of Defense
- GLBA, SOC, and the FTC Safeguards Rule: for the financial industry

Individual states may also have their own laws for regulating data protections. Until you know which of the laws apply to your business and which don't, it's far too confusing to come up with a compliance strategy.

2. Create a Compliance and Security Framework That Matches the Regulations

These laws often have overlapping requirements and rules for businesses of different sizes. Compliance and security frameworks are systems of rules and best practices that cover a broad spectrum of regulatory requirements. The two most common are NIST 800 and CIS.

The goal at this stage is to find a level of these frameworks that covers everything required to meet regulations rather than coming up with an individual plan for each law. This way, your business can focus on just one plan.

The National Institute of Standards and Technology (NIST) has created one standard of security that is used by the government. One place to start with this framework is to read NIST 800-171. This will give you a comprehensive overview of current cybersecurity best practices, along with different levels of protection.

The Center for Internet Security (CIS) recommends a set of best cyber hygiene practices called the Community Defense Model (CDM) and then adds additional benchmarks depending on your industry and regulatory requirements.

These frameworks cover a wide range of business needs, from essential best practices all the way to the most sophisticated cybersecurity protections known to research. By working with one of these frameworks, you'll know exactly what you need to do to meet the regulations. When regulations change down the road, the frameworks will give you a road map to make improvements.

Which should you choose? NIST and CIS are broadly similar, but, depending on your regulations, you may have to favor one over the other. For example, CMMC compliance requires compliance with the NIST 800 standards. The easiest way to decide if you're unsure is by working with a compliance expert.

3. Match the Regulatory Requirements to the Framework and Make a Plan

Once you know your regulatory requirements and have a framework, the next step is to plan to get compliant. The first thing is to match your regulatory requirements to the framework you've selected. The regulations will tell you what you need to do, and the framework will explain how you can meet the regulations.

This will take some time, and you will need to get agreement from management before you implement the plan. Some changes you may need to make could have major business impacts. If you just hand the requirement list to your security team on Friday and expect it to be done on Monday, you'll have a lot of angry employees!

Here's an example of how a security compliance upgrade could disrupt your business. Standard passwords are strings of characters memorized by users, but these can be stolen. Two-factor authentication (2FA) is a powerful way to reduce the chances of hackers using someone's account to break into your systems. It adds another layer of security by adding either a biometric (e.g., a fingerprint) or an object the user has that can generate a random number to the login process. It's much less likely that an attacker could obtain both factors.

2FA is a common regulatory requirement for system security, but you may have systems that cannot support it. For example, a computer in a corner running an old software package for a piece of manufacturing equipment might not support 2FA, but there's no other way to run the machine. Another obstacle could be that your employees might not have phones to receive 2FA messages. Adjusting the plan to meet challenges like these is part of the planning process.

This is just one factor you'll have to consider in order to reach compliance, and it's vital to get it right before a regulator comes knocking at your door. Any gaps in your plan could get you fined. We strongly urge you to consider working with an external compliance expert rather than trying to figure it all out on your own.

4. Implement the Plan

Once you've created your plan, it's time to implement it. The plan should include:

- Who is responsible for the implementation or parts of it (i.e., physical security vs. policy documentation vs. technical implementation).
- Who users and management can turn to if they encounter a problem.
- How employees will get notified about the changes and the timetable.
- What all the things are that need to change to get compliant.
- When each piece will be completed.
- When the entire plan will be finished.

At this point, the ball is in your court to finish what your compliance expert recommends. For a small business, it will probably take a combination of internal and external resources to do the job. Every company will be different.

Again, if you're unsure about how to implement your plan, find a trusted partner that understands how to do it. That will save you time with trial and error, and it should cost you much less than figuring out all the steps on your own.

A final step of this stage is to get an external audit of your plan to get certified for compliance. If you have already done the work and have your documented plan, you should pass your compliance test. After that, you can proudly say that your company is within regulations and tell your customers and vendors about your achievement.

5. Monitor Compliance

However, compliance is not a one-time thing! Your plan needs to be monitored over time to make sure it's still meeting changes in regulations, cybersecurity practices, attack exposure, and business changes. Your company should do this review quarterly to make sure you're not slipping out of compliance.

Also, remember that compliance is not security. Compliance will make it much harder for an attacker to get in, but one slipup of security could help an attacker walk right through the safeguards you've set up. You will need to have someone watching over cybersecurity, and they will use the tools you've provided through your compliance plan to enforce best practices and fight off attacks.

Compliance Will Save Your Company Money

Will it cost money to get compliant if you're not there yet? It's almost certain. Frankly, most businesses have terrible cybersecurity and cyber hygiene practices. It's the reason so many companies are getting hacked these days, including small businesses.

Cyberattacks target small businesses about half the time because they're often unprotected and still have valuable information that can be sold or used. A small startup might have crucial IP stolen and sold. A one-person law firm will have confidential information about their clients that would ruin their business if it got out. No matter your business size, you are a target.

The cost of a breach is far more than the cost you'll pay to get compliant. Stolen data can cost you money, reputation, and opportunities to sell your business and can make you a target of regulators fighting against cybercrime.

If all businesses met their compliance regulations and kept on top of them, cybercriminals would have a much harder time doing their dirty work. I encourage you to speak with compliance experts like my team at Affinity Tech Solutions to see what you can do to protect your business.

About Jeremy

Jeremy Valverde is the owner of Affinity Tech Solutions, LLC, an information technology services provider in Florida, offering services to small and medium-sized businesses with a focus on medical companies.

His business helps these companies become compliant with HIPAA and similar legislation to protect the information of their clients and improve the value of their businesses. Prior to founding Affinity Tech Solutions, Jeremy was the CIO of Summ-IT Healthcare Consulting Services, LLC.

Affinity Tech Solutions is an information technology services provider for small businesses in Central Florida. Their goal is to help small businesses ensure that the computers, printers, networks, smartphones, laptops, security systems, and any other part of their IT infrastructure all work properly, securely, and reliably.

For more information, contact Jeremy at Affinity Tech Solutions:

Email: jvalverde@affinitytechsolutions.com
Phone: (352) 433-4031
Web: www.affinitytechsolutions.com
LinkedIn: www.linkedin.com/in/jeremy-valverde-9444068/

Chapter 21

THE SECRET TO MITIGATING YOUR RISK
Roland Parker

S o many people say, "I don't need to worry about security or compliance—we're too small. I just want somebody to support my business in case something goes wrong."

Sorry, but the cyberthreat landscape for small to medium-sized businesses has completely changed. While attacks on BIG companies headline the nightly news, it's small business owners who represent the low-hanging fruit for the hackers.

Criminals operating out of Russia, China, and Eastern Europe absolutely love to go after American businesses under $50 million in revenue. Accenture's cybercrime study revealed that nearly 43% of cyberattacks targeted small and medium-sized businesses (SMBs)—and they're easy targets because most don't have proper security or proper backups. (The Accenture study further revealed that only 14% of targeted SMBs were prepared to handle such attacks.)[77]

The most likely reason you don't hear about small companies getting hit is that they either paid the ransom or went out of business because they couldn't recover the data.

Similarly, I find a lot of business owners don't understand the very real and significant value of compliance. They think it's just a big, long laundry list of rules you follow so you don't get fined. But what they don't appreciate is that following those rules can make your whole operation more secure, which matters a great deal to your business—in fact, now more than ever.

Because when you're attacked, it goes way beyond having to deal with an annoying, temporary shutdown: It's not just your data that's compromised; it's also your credibility. Critical client information is now exposed and available on the dark web. You could end up losing clients and revenue because it now appears your company can no longer be trusted.

If you're a smaller company providing a product or service to a larger company, we've seen where they simply aren't willing to deal with you if you can't show you have your systems and infrastructure in compliance. Unless you can prove that you're doing all these things to keep yourself secure, larger companies and organizations will take their business elsewhere.

So, small companies are now finding they HAVE to get more in line with compliance and security just because the companies they serve don't want to be associated with those added risks.

Fortunately, there are several steps you can take now to safeguard your business and data.

Key Things You Can Do to Reduce Your Risk

The first step is to complete a *risk assessment* for your organization, from disaster recovery to cybersecurity. By this, I mean taking an in-depth, step-by-step assessment of your entire operation to identify where you and your data are most at risk. A proper risk assessment should include:

- Scope of the evaluation—you can assess a particular department or unit, or your entire organization.
- Identification of the physical and logical assets included in that scope as well as the primary threats to those assets.
- Potential impact of a cyberattack, typically rated as high, medium, or low.
- Risk rating calculation obtained by factoring the potential impact of a risk based on the likelihood it will actually happen.
- Documentation of risks to ensure your organization has a solid grasp of the challenges it faces.

You'll want to create an *incident response plan*, also known as an IRP. Its purpose is to help your organization BEFORE, DURING, and AFTER a confirmed or suspected security incident. At a minimum, you'll want to identify critical systems and potential risks and clearly define the roles and responsibilities of everyone on your incident response team. Once completed, the IRP needs to be reviewed, tested, and fully integrated into your corporate training process.

Make sure to focus on *employee training*—the majority of issues companies face are typically caused by employees, either unwittingly or simply as a result of mistakes. According to the World Economic Forum, human error accounts for 95% of cybersecurity breaches.[78] This highlights the importance of employee training and awareness. It's critical to invest not only in training your employees to understand the risks, but also in testing them in various ways to ensure they're doing things correctly.

Along with your employees, you'll need to ensure that all your *vendors* are compliant and have redundancy plans in place for what they provide to you.

No matter how good you are at putting up defenses, criminals can always find a way in—what matters, therefore, is how quickly you can detect and remediate to isolate the issue and kick them out. That's why it's critical to have multiple layers of security and backups, as well as to make sure you continuously *monitor and protect your network*.

You'll especially want to enforce the use of *strong passwords* that get changed regularly—a good password manager is essential in today's environment, as is the use of multifactor authentication. And because the bad guys are always trying to find new ways to get inside your network and workplace, be diligent in regularly installing *security patches and updates* to keep your software and hardware up-to-date and reduce vulnerability.

In the event something bad does happen, you'll want to protect yourself by having in place a solid *backup system*—both off-site and on-site—that's incremental as well as image-based. Determine how quickly you can get back up and running if you were to suffer a disaster and ensure that you can run in the cloud should your premises be inaccessible. (Don't forget to consider *data retention*—some companies, like CPAs, may need to go as far back as eighteen months.) Make sure you're testing backups regularly to ensure they're running correctly.s

Don't overlook the need to do everything you can to ensure the *physical security* of your operations and data, which means restricting access to certain areas, as well as disabling USB ports, security cameras, and even the actual doors to the rooms themselves.

Finally, you'll want to ensure you're *compliant* with the regulations associated with your industry. It's essential to be aware of what compliance regulations affect your industry. Make certain to put the correct policies and procedures in place before something bad happens. By doing so, not only are you protecting yourself against liability and huge fines but you're also making yourself more secure, which lowers your overall risk.

Trust but Verify

It's important that you ask any potential MSP how they plan to handle compliance and security, especially when facing different scenarios. For example:

- What would happen if I got hit with ransomware?
- What would happen if I got hit by fire? Or flooding?
- What if we had a lightning surge that took out all my computers?

After asking if they've thought through dealing with these and other challenges, then ask the critical question:

"After that happens, how quickly can I be back up and running?"

Getting up and running ASAP is so important. During COVID, I recall a situation with one client who had employees remoting in from home. They got hit with ransomware and had to shut down about thirty-five seats. Fortunately, we had a plan in place, along with secure and timely backups. Within just eight hours, we had them back up and running as if nothing had happened.

Go through different disaster scenarios and figure out what you would do if that happened to you and how quickly you could be back up and running.

When choosing someone to work with, you don't want to get left holding the bag if they can't deliver what was promised. Make sure your IT provider reports on a quarterly basis to show:

- Backups have been consistently run and tested.
- Penetration tests have made sure everything's secure from the inside and the outside.
- Your computers are in good health, noting any that need to be replaced or upgraded.

Never simply assume everything's okay just because they've said so.

Think about it—if you're NOT getting those kinds of reports, can you really trust them?

I always say it's a great thing to trust. But make sure you're getting reports proving they're doing what they say they're doing. When we started doing backups for people, we made sure everything was securely backed up. Because without a quality backup, there's no guarantee that, even if you paid a ransom, you're going to get your data back.

Without having these security systems and processes in place, you're literally at the mercy of anyone who somehow manages to get through. And the last thing you want to discover after experiencing an attack is that the backup data wasn't there or was somehow corrupted.

So, don't just trust—trust but verify.

The Threats to Your Business Are Only Going to Grow

Cybercrime continues to be a great way to make tons of money, and hacking is a multibillion-dollar industry. We're going to see increased attacks coming from places like Russia and China, which have an agenda against US-based businesses. The situation is only going to get worse.

The companies that make the effort to achieve compliance and put security policies and systems in place are going to have a leg up on competitors who don't. Anyone who doesn't invest the necessary time and money in cloud infrastructure, backup, and security will inevitably fall by the wayside.

Because when disaster strikes—and it will—they're not going to make it. The costs of an attack can be staggering and will hit you in different ways.

- First, there's the cost of investigation and repair of the hardware and software, which can range from $10,000 to $50,000 or more.
- Then, when compliance is required, you could face fines ranging from $10,000 up to $100,000.
- Of course, there's the ransom itself, which can run to tens of thousands of dollars.
- Finally, there's the cost to your reputation, including lost customers and future opportunities.

The final bill can be enormous and, frankly, devastating to any company not adequately prepared.

That's why it's so important for every business, no matter its size, to put those security systems in place NOW. Even if you can't do everything, do something. Don't wait until something bad happens. That could mean the end of your business.

Make Sure to Get the Help You Need

As a business owner, you're constantly facing several different risks relative to your company's systems, network, and data.

- You could experience data loss through equipment failure, surges, storms, floods, fire, and theft.
- Disgruntled employees could commit sabotage or even a single employee error could cause major problems.
- Ransomware, phishing, and other cyberattacks are a constant threat.

The sad reality is that only 52% of companies can recover from severe data loss. So, like it or not, if you're in business today, you HAVE to take cybersecurity seriously.

Yes, it can be a significant challenge. But help is available.

We have been assisting companies in the Houston market since 2003. We specialize in both cybersecurity and rapid response proactive IT support. We're locally based and monitor companies' networks on a 24/7 basis. We always answer our phones live, and because we keep a wide range of inventory on hand, we can offer an amazingly quick turnaround on most issues. Our customers love our personal service and friendly, no-tech jargon, which is demonstrated by over 500 five-star reviews on Google.

One thing we offer is a free dark web scan to let you know if your personal information is out there on the dark web.

Now, you might wonder, "If it's there, what do I do about it?" As they say, knowledge is power, and once you know a problem exists, you can take immediate corrective action:

- If you discover that passwords have been compromised, change those passwords.
- If your credit card information is on the dark web, get your credit card changed before it becomes even more widespread.
- If your Social Security number has been compromised, you may have to set up some type of monitoring alert.

The important thing is to be proactive. Check to see if your information is on the dark web. If you've got dark web monitoring, it'll alert you when things happen.

We offer the first dark web scan for free so if you discover you've been compromised, you can then do something about it.

We also offer a free network assessment that will examine your systems and let you know where they're vulnerable from an internal point of view, along with penetration tests to determine the vulnerability of the network externally.

And whether you use us or not, we're going to give you those reports so you can know there are specific actions you need to take to make your company secure.

There's no charge, no risk. It's our gift to you.

About Roland

For over twenty years, Impress Computers has been supporting Houston-based businesses, specializing in both cybersecurity and rapid response proactive IT support.

Roland and Mandy Parker originally founded Impress Computers in Zimbabwe in 1994, quickly growing the company to become one of the nation's largest IT firms.

Due to political unrest in Zimbabwe in the early 2000s, they began looking for a new location. After searching a world map, they discovered the suburban gem of Katy, Texas. Moving quickly, they formed a US company, signed a five-year lease, and organized visas for themselves along with some key staff members.

In 2013, they became US citizens, and in 2015, they were able to purchase their new building on Provincial Boulevard in Katy.

Impress Computers now employs fifteen staff members dedicated to providing high-level custom IT support to businesses in Houston and surrounding areas. They are 100% committed to making sure business owners have the most reliable and professional IT service in the Greater Houston area.

Over the years, Roland has seen many companies struggle with ransomware attacks and the loss of critical data. He's made it his personal mission to provide security, backups, and peace of mind to his business owner customers—making sure they've got the training and tools to handle whatever situations arise.

From 1996 to 2000, Roland attended the Institute of Chartered Secretaries and Administrators (now the Chartered Governance Institute), focusing on leadership and governance. Both Roland and Mandy love Formula One racing, and the new track in Austin is only a couple of hours away.

For more information, contact Roland at Impress Computers:

Email: info@impresscomputers.com
Phone: (281) 944-3983
Web: www.impresscomputers.tech

Chapter 22

THE TEN STRATEGIES YOU MUST HAVE IN PLACE BEFORE INSURERS WILL EVEN CONSIDER WRITING A CYBER POLICY
Michael Mullin

This isn't 2022's cyber insurance landscape. Coverage now looks a lot different, and here's a hint: It's not pretty. Given the broadening reach and impact of cybercrime, cyber insurance is urgently becoming a priority for C-suites. A few years ago, getting a cybersecurity liability policy was as easy as signing up for car insurance with zero points on your license. Piece of cake. Now, expect every crumb on that slice to be scrutinized.

With the unprecedented number of companies looking for coverage amid fear of more frequent and increasingly sophisticated cyberattacks, insurance carriers are licking their wounds after substantial losses from cyber claims over the last few years. In the past three years, claims have risen by 100% annually. The number of claims closed with payment grew by 200% annually over the same period.[79] The increase in demand and the direct-loss ratios have left insurers with little desire for the risk. That's why companies can expect to see continued premium increases and much stricter underwriting requirements—if you're lucky. Some businesses will be outright denied a policy if the risk is too great.

Now, you probably think that getting cyber insurance or a renewal policy with favorable premiums and coverage in today's market might seem next to impossible. It's not. IF you have what carriers seek, including healthy security controls and recovery plans. A carrier wants to be sure that a business is committed to doing all it can to prevent an attack. Are *you*?

To prove you have your house in order before you ever start shopping for cyber insurance, here are ten essential security infrastructures and tools you MUST have in place to help increase your credibility with carriers.

1. Antivirus Software

All computers should have antivirus software and antispyware installed to help prevent, search for, detect, and remove software viruses and other types of malware. These security programs look for patterns based on the signatures or behaviors of known malware. Antivirus vendors find new and updated malware daily, so it is CRITICAL that you install the latest updates on your computers to protect against emerging threats.

2. MFA and PAM

Insurers are looking more closely at how multifactor authentication is used after realizing that many organizations have not fully implemented MFA within their networks. MFA, also called 2FA, assures that only authenticated users can access your network.

Moreover, special focus is currently being placed on "privileged accounts" that safeguard vital data. These accounts are typically managed by system administrators, yet they often lack associated users. For those types of privileged accounts, underwriters have started making privileged access management (PAM) mandatory to create an extra layer of security and isolate high-value assets from potential threats or vulnerabilities. PAM provides easy and secure privileged access for all third-party vendors maintaining and supporting your company's IT system from outside the company network.

3. Network Firewall

Your company's network must be protected using a firewall. A firewall is often the first line of defense in your network's security. It monitors incoming and outgoing network traffic, checking for IP addresses, content types, and other rules, and then permits or blocks it, depending on the security protocols you put in place.

A firewall device can be hardware, software, or cloud-based and is used between your secure private network and the Internet or other networks to reduce the risk of cyberattacks and prevent unauthorized access.

4. Backup and Recovery

Cyber insurers are paying much closer attention to a business's data integrity, strength, and recoverability. Regular backups protect you against potentially catastrophic ransomware attacks, saving your business time and money. It could mean the difference between having to pay a ransom to unlock your data—and there are still no guarantees they'll unlock it anyway—and being able to reject the ransom demand and restore your backup files.

If a regulatory body doesn't dictate the frequency of your backups, I would highly suggest using a 3-2-1-1-0 backup strategy to ensure multiple copies of data are backed up and retained in the event of a cyberattack:

- Keep three different copies of the data. Retain the original copy, along with at least two more backups.
- Store backups on at least two different media (e.g., one on an internal hard disk drive and one on removable storage media).
- Keep at least one copy of data at an off-site location.
- Maintain at least one copy offline (not connected) so hackers can't access it.
- Make sure your backups are verified and have zero errors.

Backup and recovery strategies shouldn't be on autopilot. Your business should perform periodic tests to pinpoint deficiencies and make changes as needed, especially if your data changes frequently. Being able to quickly recover and restore your data in the event of a cyberattack or hardware failure minimizes the time lost, even if the network goes down.

5. Endpoint Detection and Response

Endpoints—the physical devices connected to your network, from laptops and desktops to smartphones—are easy access points for cybercriminals. It is critical that organizations implement a layered approach to cybersecurity, including endpoint detection and response (EDR and XDR) software tools that provide surveillance of every endpoint to detect and remediate possible breaches. While these tools are essential components of a security defense system, sophisticated adversaries have found a way to shut off or avoid these controls by exploiting administrative credentials.

To combat this potential vulnerability, cyber insurers increasingly demand endpoint privilege control measures, including removing local admin rights from all users in an organization. Finding the balance between providing sufficient protection and not compromising operational efficiency is now paramount for defending against cyberthreats looming on the horizon.

6. Security Awareness Training

Ransomware, password cracking, and phishing. These are all real threats to today's businesses, no matter what size you are, and they're getting more dangerous and calculated by the minute as bad actors get smarter and faster. If everyone on your staff—from your interns to your CEO to your IT team—isn't on the same security page, you are putting your entire organization at risk.

A proper security awareness training program reinforces the role each team member plays in helping to prevent successful cyberattacks and the consequences of unsafe and risky online behavior. Security awareness training helps employees identify security risks like phishing emails and websites and makes reporting suspicious activity easier. According to a study by IBM, 95% of cybersecurity breaches in 2022 resulted from human error.[80] In the eyes of a cyber insurance provider, security awareness training isn't limited to an annual meeting; it should become part of your corporate culture.

7. IR Process and Testing

As cyber incidents increase, more insurers want to see that you have an incident response (IR) plan in place. But it's not enough to check off the box that indicates you have a plan. It needs to be actionable, readily practiced, and frequently refined to give you the confidence to survive a cyberattack. A sound cyber incident response plan should include these key elements:

- Outline of all appropriate internal stakeholders' response roles.
- Instructions for contacting outside response experts.
- Response protocols dictated by the cyber insurance carrier.
- Best practices for dealing with cyberthreats.
- Ready accessibility in the event of a cyber incident.

8. Patch Management

Another best practice frequently required by cyber insurers is a comprehensive patch management process. Patches can help address vulnerabilities that attackers may target by modifying operating systems and software to improve security, fix bugs, and improve features and performance.

Regularly installing patches is one of the best practices to ensure your devices and software are not vulnerable to known security issues against fast-moving cyberthreats. Here's a patch management strategy I recommend to my clients.

- Establish a baseline inventory of your production systems.
- Categorize and group each asset by risk and priority.
- Test the patch stability.
- Determine which endpoints need to be patched.
- Pilot deploy a sample patch to verify its safety.
- Document the state of your systems before and after a patch is applied.

9. Vulnerability Management

Similar to patch management, but not quite the same, vulnerability management identifies, scans, prioritizes, mitigates, and repairs vulnerabilities for remediation, whereas patch management applies patches to vulnerable systems. Both play their part in improving your business's overall security posture and can help you get a gold star from cyber insurance providers.

Vulnerability management is an ongoing and proactive process to reduce a business's overall risk exposure by mitigating as many vulnerabilities as possible. There are typically five stages in the vulnerability workflow:

1. Discovery
2. Categorization and prioritization
3. Resolution
4. Reassessment
5. Reporting

10. Supplier Risk Strategy

Let's face it: Many companies today rely on vendors and third-party partners to help their businesses grow and stay competitive, making it unbelievably challenging to eliminate the cyber risks that may come along with an interconnected supply chain. Remember the SolarWinds hack in 2020? That supply chain breach is unprecedented and one of the largest—if not the largest—ever recorded.[81] While you can't possibly eliminate the risks that occur through your suppliers, you can and should develop a strategy for minimizing those risks.

As cyber concerns have exposed other supplier risk issues, it's essential to assess and monitor your suppliers to ensure they aren't the weakest link in your business's security posture. Here are some questions developed by the National Institute of Standards and Technology to help you determine how risky a supplier's cybersecurity practices may be.

- Is the vendor's software and hardware design process documented? Repeatable? Measurable?
- Is the mitigation of known vulnerabilities factored into product design (through product architecture, run-time protection techniques, and code review)?
- How does the vendor stay current on emerging vulnerabilities?
- What controls are in place to manage and monitor production processes?
- How well do suppliers vet their own personnel?
- How well do the vendors vet their service providers?
- How well do the vendors vet their products and software?

Conclusion

Tougher questions, greater security practices, higher premiums, less favorable terms, higher retention fees, increased renewal rejections, and flat-out denials. These are some things you can expect when you apply for or renew a cybersecurity insurance policy this coming year.

Given how hard it is to get cyber insurance, you may ask yourself, "Is it worth it?" If your business uses computers and mobile devices, accepts credit cards or other digital payment types, or keeps and stores confidential customer data, the answer is YES.

Best advice: Don't go it alone. Getting a favorable policy depends on your underwriter questionnaire and pre-assessment being done correctly. Working with an MSP with expert cybersecurity capabilities can help you navigate the grueling process and ensure you have all ten and more strategies in place.

About Michael

Michael Mullin is the president and CEO of Integrated Business Systems, Inc., a managed IT and cybersecurity services provider serving northern New Jersey and New York City businesses since 1979.

IBS specializes in delivering business technology solutions to real estate companies. With diversified backgrounds in property management, accounting, and systems, its talented group of consultants works with new and existing customers to ensure they maximize their use of IBS software.

Michael has more than forty years of experience in the technology industry. Since 1987, he has witnessed how technology empowers small and midsize companies to make employees more productive, deliver services to customers, present information more meaningfully, and create better business outcomes. Prior to joining IBS in 2010, Michael worked with high-profile organizations, including Yardi Systems, First Advantage/SafeRent, and Geac Computer Corporation, where he focused on property operations, construction, and accounting.

As CEO, Michael ensures IBS clients use available technologies to their fullest advantage while remaining safe and secure. As cybercrime has grown from being a nuisance to potentially destroying a lifetime of work in minutes, he has made cybersecurity his mission. He teaches and informs business owners and operators of small and midsize businesses about the perils of these threat actors and how companies can protect themselves.

Michael attended Western Illinois University and the New York Institute of Finance from 1974 to 1979. He has completed various professional-level programs over his forty-five-year career. He is also an Acumatica MVP, recognized for being at the forefront of ERP innovation and cloud knowledge. Michael has sat on the board of directors for the National Multifamily Housing Council and has held membership in the Suppliers Council of the National Apartment Association.

He co-authored and published the My Desk Top Coach series, a personal and professional development tool that integrates with one-on-one help desk coaching and allows employees to learn best practices and customer support skills at their own pace and in their own time.

Michael, an entertaining and knowledgeable speaker, regularly addresses local and online professional associations, business groups, and Chamber of Commerce groups that serve the small and midsize business market in or near Totowa, New Jersey. Additionally, he is frequently invited to radio, television, and podcast interviews, as well as roundtable or panel discussions.

When Michael isn't busy helping IBS's clients keep their systems current, safe, and ahead of the competition, he enjoys spending time with his family, including eight grandchildren. He's also an avid golfer and is involved in several projects that serve his church and community, including those helping people transition from bad situations onto paths of stability.

For more information, contact Michael at Integrated Business Systems:

Email: mmullin@ibsre.com
Phone: (973) 949-0347
Web: www.ibsre.com
LinkedIn: www.linkedin.com/in/mikemullin
Address: 999 Riverview Dr., Totowa, NJ 07512

Chapter 23

CRITICAL STEPS TO TAKE IF YOU'VE BEEN HACKED

Daaniël van Siereveld

If you don't think you're a target for hackers, they have you right where they want you. At some point, most companies will experience a hack or data breach. While a hack doesn't always mean the hackers get away with anything, it will embolden them to try again. Eventually, if you don't shore up the leaks, they will get away with your data or your customers' data. A 2022 survey of security leaders reported that 79% of their organizations experienced a ransomware attack.[82] This should worry every business. And if you're a small to medium-sized business (SMB), you're no exception. It's estimated that 43% of cyberattacks target SMBs. Even worse, 60% of SMBs that experience a data breach go out of business within six months.[83]

I know that some of those statistics are scary, and you're wondering if it's worth trying. I don't tell you these numbers to discourage you from starting or running a business but to prepare you for the realities that today's SMBs face. You should do everything you can to prevent a breach but also prepare for the likelihood it could happen. If you just put your head in the sand and think it won't happen to you, then you won't be prepared to respond when it does. Planning your response to a hack is exactly what we're going to discuss in this chapter.

You've Been Hacked—Now What?

The emotions are overwhelming upon realizing you've been hacked or are in the middle of a hack. Therefore, have a plan in place before it occurs. This helps take emotions out of it, and you can immediately start your response. If you don't have a plan, then you're likely to spin out of control or freeze up. Your employees don't need to see you huddled in the corner of your office in the fetal position, mumbling to yourself about how you should have been a park ranger. So, let's put together a plan to keep that scene from ever playing out.

I'll outline the steps, and then we'll go over each of them in more detail. Depending on the size of your organization, some of these steps may not be necessary or may need to be outsourced to an expert. I'll go through all the steps, and you decide if your team can handle them. The plan is to identify, isolate, assemble, engage, preserve, assess, implement, notify, analyze, and enhance.

Identify the Hack

The first step, of course, is to identify and confirm that a hack has occurred. You don't want to spend time and money if you can verify there hasn't been a hack. Start with these questions: Why do you think there has been a breach? Did someone click on a link in an email and report it? Did you notice some files are missing from a server? Does your network seem slower than usual? If you know where it started, then you can focus your efforts. If you don't, then look for signs of unusual system behavior or unauthorized access. You can usually accomplish this by analyzing the logs.

In an ideal world, you have a security information and event management solution. A SIEM is a way to collect logs from various systems, allowing them to be queried more easily, which makes it easier to identify threats. Many SIEMs will identify threats proactively. If you don't have a SIEM, you'll need to go through logs on each system and network device. Consider the following logs for analysis:

- Operating system logs for servers and client machines. Look for failed login attempts, password changes, services being started or stopped, and elevated access as the root or admin user. Then run a command using sudo.
- Application logs such as web applications, web servers, and databases. For databases, look for failed logins or commands that pull all data from tables. For web servers, look for things like attempts to access pages that don't exist or injected SQL or code in the URL. Look for similar things in the application logs.
- Antivirus or other security logs. Make sure antivirus software hasn't been disabled or updates turned off. Check logs that monitor change detection.

- Logs related to networks like firewalls and DNS servers. Look for excessive traffic or large amounts of data being moved outside of the network. Look for high traffic volume that is being blocked by the firewall and check if any rules were recently added or removed. Also, check for administrator access on these devices.

Isolate and Secure Affected Systems

As soon as you confirm the breach and you know where it originated, isolate that system from the rest of the network. If hackers compromised a specific account, change the password or disable the account immediately. It's a good time to consider multifactor authentication as well, especially for privileged accounts. If you're a small business and you know there has been a breach but are not sure where it came from, you may have to take the drastic action of disconnecting from the Internet completely. This will at least stop the hackers from communicating with your systems.

Assemble the Incident Response Team

Put together a response team with representatives from IT, security, legal, public relations, and executive management. You should already have a good idea of whom to include before an incident occurs, but there may be some changes depending on the type of incident. This team will oversee the response, coordinate efforts, and ensure a comprehensive approach to addressing the incident.

Engage External Expertise

If you're a small business, you may not have the in-house expertise to handle all aspects of a breach. There is no shame in asking for help. Your data, money, customers, and reputation are at stake. Investigate firms ahead of time. Do your homework and find a vendor that meets your needs and fills in the missing parts of your IT security team. You don't want to wait until you're in the middle of a hack to vet a new service provider. Make sure the vendor has cybersecurity or incident response experts. Their specialized skills can help identify vulnerabilities, contain breaches, and guide your organization through the recovery process.

Preserve Evidence

Preserve and document evidence related to the hack. This includes capturing screenshots, logs, system snapshots, and any other information that may aid in identifying the source and extent of the breach. Proper evidence collection is crucial for potential legal proceedings and internal investigations. Look in logs for Internet protocol (IP) addresses and other items that may identify the hacker or their location. Larger companies with experienced cybersecurity teams may want to leave affected systems on the network until they can trace the hackers. For most companies, containment is going to be more important than evidence, so base this on your team's abilities and whether you think the hackers have already retrieved the data they were after.

Assess the Impact

Conduct a thorough assessment of the breach's impact. Understanding the scope and severity of the attack will guide your response efforts and help prioritize actions. You'll need to answer the following questions to know the full impact:

- Did the hackers get away with data?
- What type of data was stolen?
- Are financial systems impacted?
- Are customers affected, and if so, how?
- Are there any compliance violations?

Implement Containment and Recovery Measures

Now that you know where the breach came from and you've isolated the affected systems or credentials, it's time to work with your incident response team to develop a plan for containment and recovery. This may include patching, upgrading unsupported software, removing malware, and restoring data from backups. If you were the victim of a ransomware attack, you may need off-site backups delivered, as hackers often try to encrypt your backup files and live data. We'll discuss it in more detail later, but you should also start thinking about the steps needed to keep it from happening again.

Notify Relevant Parties

Comply with all legal and regulatory requirements. For example, if you handle certain types of data, such as health care data, then you'll need to follow the requirements set forth under HIPAA regulations. You should also contact customers, employees, partners, and other stakeholders. Prompt and transparent communication could be the key to staying in business. Provide detailed information about the breach, its impact, and the steps taken to address the breach. Consult legal counsel to ensure compliance with applicable laws and contracts. It's also a good idea to report the breach to the proper authorities. You can report the incident to your local FBI field office or make an online complaint with the Internet Crime Complaint Center at www.ic3.gov.

Conduct a Post-Incident Analysis

You need to conduct a post-incident analysis and review after any hack. This should happen after you've contained the breach and restored your systems. Take this opportunity to identify the root cause. Was this from a phishing or social engineering campaign? Was it a zero-day attack because you're running unsupported software versions? Was it a weakness in your security infrastructure? Avoid finger-pointing and the blame game. This won't resolve anything and will just cause rifts, which tends to make people stop sharing information. You need everyone to be open during the analysis without fear of reprisals.

Enhance Security Measures

Now that your analysis is complete, it's time to use the lessons you learned to improve your security posture. If you found out the breach started with a phishing email, you probably need to improve or increase the frequency of your cybersecurity training. If the hack resulted from a zero-day vulnerability, you should set a cadence for patching and upgrading your systems. It should be part of a regular schedule. If user credentials were compromised, tighten access controls, password rotation, and auditing. No matter what led to the breach, implement encryption for sensitive data and increase auditing to be proactive in checking for anomalies in the future.

Conclusion

Running a business is hard enough without the fear of cyberattacks, but they are a reality. Take proactive steps to prevent cyberattacks but prepare for the real possibility that it can happen. If you use these steps to create a detailed plan, you'll be ahead of the game. Work with your IT, cybersecurity, legal, and executive teams to define the details for each of these steps and create a written plan. Do some research and have meetings with cybersecurity experts. They can give you an unbiased security review to make sure you're doing your best to keep the hackers out. Once you have a trusted provider, you can keep them on speed dial if a breach occurs.

About Daaniël

Daaniël van Siereveld is the founder, owner, and CEO of Issue53 LLC, a managed services provider helping businesses manage their IT needs so they can focus on the core functions of their business. A heavy focus on cybersecurity and networking puts Issue53 in a great position to help businesses improve their cybersecurity posture and get them back online in the event of a hack. Issue53 has strong skills in cloud-native technologies as well, and they believe compliance should be a priority for every business.

Daaniël has been fixing and tinkering with things his entire life. For his sixteenth birthday, instead of asking his parents for a car, he begged them for a 16-port switch so he could set up his own network. That curiosity and ingenuity led to an opportunity while in high school. He was offered the chance to learn at Cisco, and that opportunity changed the direction of his life. Daaniël was bored by subjects other than science and technology, and his teachers could see it. His boredom was a thing of the past at Cisco. His brain was a sponge, and it was never full.

After high school, Daaniël attended college in Portland, Oregon, earning a Bachelor of Science in data communication systems technology. While he was there, he landed a job as a contractor at a major chip manufacturer, where he gained valuable insight into his career and life. After that job, he knew he didn't want to work for a large corporation again. He had felt like a number and didn't feel he could make a difference. Also, while in college, he got involved in an annual gaming event called PDXLAN in Portland. He started working at the event as a security guard to make some extra money. The second year, he worked at the event as the network admin assistant. By his third year at PDXLAN, Daaniël was the director of networking. The complexity and challenges were alluring, and he continued to work the event each year well after college. Over the years, Daaniël has appeared in several articles focused on the complexity of setting up the network for this large-scale gaming event.

Daaniël has worked for several start-ups and MSPs over the years. His last job was as the VP of IT Operations at a start-up in the digital-custody banking space. The recent bank closings put a hold on their latest round of investment funds, and everyone was laid off, so it was time to make his move. With the experience he gained from working at other MSPs over the years, Daaniël knew he was ready to run his own shop, and the company shutdown was just the push he needed.

When Daaniël isn't working, you can find him spending time with his wife and two young children. He never wants his kids to wonder if he'll show up for one of their events, so he makes family a priority and encourages his employees to do the same. If the weather is right, you'll find Daaniël riding his motorcycle. An avid motorcyclist and admitted adrenaline junkie, he won't be found sitting still very often.

For more information, contact Daaniël at Issue53:

Email: Daaniël.vanSiereveld@Issue53.com
Phone: (971) 394-3878
Web: www.issue53.com

Chapter 24

UNDERSTANDING CMMC COMPLIANCE: WHAT YOU NEED TO KNOW
Craig Rabe

C MMC stands for Cybersecurity Maturity Model Certification. In the most basic explanation, it's a set of rules and guidelines that companies must follow if they want to work with the Department of Defense and keep the United States' military secrets safe. CMMC makes sure these companies are doing their best to protect important information. By following the CMMC rules, we can make sure the military's secrets stay secret, and the bad guys don't get their hands on them. As a business owner, it's crucial to understand CMMC so you know if and how it applies to you and what you need to do. While it would be impossible to spell out everything about CMMC in a book, let alone a chapter, some basics will give you a good understanding and enough information to get you headed in the right direction.

What Is CMMC?

CMMC is a US Department of Defense program designed to protect sensitive information. If your business plans to work with the DoD or its contractors, you'll need to comply with CMMC guidelines. These guidelines consist of various cybersecurity and other practices that help ensure the safety of valuable data. By obtaining CMMC certification, you demonstrate your commitment to securing critical information, which is required for you to bid on DoD contacts. It can also make your business more attractive to potential clients and partners within the defense industry. Additionally, adhering to CMMC requirements helps protect your own business against cyberthreats and data breaches.

The DoD launched CMMC 2.0 to increase the trust in organizations working with the department. It applies to defense industrial base (DIB) contractors and has three levels of certification: Foundational, Advanced, and Expert. This unified standard measures and certifies cybersecurity requirements, helping to ensure the safety of important data and resources. By implementing CMMC, the DoD is taking steps toward safeguarding its supply chain from potential cyberthreats.

Why Is CMMC Needed?

The short story of why CMMC is needed is that our national security was at risk.

Prior to CMMC, the US government relied on subcontractors to protect their own cybersecurity and assess themselves, but this did not always happen. As a result, intellectual property that took decades and billions of dollars to develop has been continuously stolen by foreign governments.

Military experts fear that countries such as Russia and China are making concerted efforts to diminish US superiority. Using stolen intel, they are closing the gap, which could lead to problems with the US's ability to defend allies. Whatever these countries can't develop on their own, they steal through cyberspace.

China, for example, is focused on building its own capabilities and challenging those of the United States. They've demonstrated they are willing to get their hands on advanced weapons technology through all sorts of means, including stealing secrets from US defense contractors.

In 2018, Chinese government hackers compromised the computers of a US Navy contractor and stole 614 gigabytes of highly sensitive data related to undersea warfare and a closely held project known as "Sea Dragon." Material stolen included signals, sensor data, submarine radio room information relating to cryptographic systems, and the Navy submarine development unit's electronic warfare library.

The data stolen was considered classified but was housed on a contractor's unclassified network. This is just one example of what raised concerns about overseeing contractors tasked with developing classified equipment such as cutting-edge weapons.

In response to the wide-scale compromise and exfiltration of defense information, the DoD released CMMC version 1.0 in January 2020. (The security requirements to protect the confidentiality of Controlled Unclassified Information [CUI] that is in CMMC has been in DoD contracts since 2017.) In November 2021, the DoD announced CMMC 2.0, an updated program structure and requirements to achieve their primary goals of safeguarding sensitive information and protecting the US.

Who Needs It?

CMMC is designed for organizations and businesses that work directly or indirectly with the US Department of Defense or its contractors. This includes manufacturers, service providers, and suppliers.

As a Business Owner, What Is Important for Me to Know About CMMC?

1. **There are three levels of security.** Previously, CMMC included five levels of security maturity, ranging from basic cyber hygiene (Level 1) to highly advanced (Level 5). The latest CMMC 2.0 model has three levels. These are Level 1 (Foundational), Level 2 (Advanced) and Level 3 (Expert). The level required for your company depends on the type of work you perform with the DoD. These majority levels include (and add to) the 110 security requirements in NIST SP 800-171 already required under DFARS 252.204-7012.

2. **It's essential to know what CMMC level you need to conduct business.** By the end of 2025, the DoD will require all contractors to be certified in one of the three CMMC levels. If a supplier is not certified at the specified level, the company cannot bid on DoD business. Determining the level needed by your company depends on the type of data exchanged or created by the DoD contract. There are three broad categories:
   - Public information is described as data that is "public release approved" and does not require any special handling or controls. Companies handling only public information will not require CMMC certification.
   - Federal Contract Information (FCI) is information that is not intended for public release. This is typically indicated in the contract. If a DoD contractor only requires FCI data as part of defense work being performed, they will probably need a Level 1 CMMC certification. Level 1 includes seventeen cybersecurity practices and allows for an annual self-assessment.

- Controlled Unclassified Information (CUI) is FCI that comes with additional guidance related to special safeguarding or handling controls. If a contractor does work for the DoD that includes sharing and processing CUI data, the organization is required to achieve at least a CMMC Level 2 certification. This level requires compliance with 110 practices in Levels 1 and 2.

3. **This is not a box-checking exercise.** Achieving CMMC compliance requires implementing various security controls and practices, such as access control, incident response, and risk management. CMMC certification requires a third-party audit that measures the maturity of a company's cybersecurity capabilities. To win DoD contracts, you must meet these requirements.

4. **CMMC is not a one-time process.** CMMC certification must be renewed every three years, and ongoing monitoring and assessment of security practices are necessary to maintain compliance.

5. **Working with an MSP/MSSP that specializes in CMMC is recommended.** The process of assessing and implementing practices, plans, and procedures to satisfy CMMC requirements is a huge project. While large prime contractors are likely to have the resources to prepare for CMMC, approximately 99% of the defense industrial base is composed of small businesses, which do not have the internal resources required to meet CMMC on their own.[84]

   In fact, smaller businesses are found to be more deficient in mature cybersecurity practices—including user authentication, network defenses, vulnerability scanning, software patching, and security information and event management (SIEM)—and cyberattack response than their larger peers. Therefore, to prepare for CMMC guidelines and meet the requirements, many companies, especially smaller DIB firms, may find it cost- and time-effective to work with a third-party services provider like an MSP or MSSP.

6. **It's essential to assess your business requirements.** Certain work with the DoD requires meeting more stringent requirements. For example, Microsoft came out with Government Community Cloud High (GCC High), a specialized cloud environment specifically designed for US government agencies and their contractors, including DoD contractors. It provides advanced security features and compliance standards designed to protect sensitive data such as CUI. But it's going to come with a hefty price tag. However, if your

work with the DoD doesn't involve handling CUI or doesn't require these more stringent requirements, you may not need GCC High. In those cases, you could explore a different cloud solution that still offers robust security but is tailored to your needs at a more affordable price tag. An assessment will help you know what you need so you can invest in the right tools and determine the right course of action to take.

7. **Self-assessment is a good place to start; however, a third-party assessment is required for CMMC compliance.** Initial scores can be obtained via a self-assessment to help you determine what your current situation is and what needs to be done to get CMMC compliant. While you can do this self-assessment yourself, most people will find it extremely difficult because they aren't likely to understand many of the items on the assessment. Therefore, it will be helpful to find a third-party Registered Practitioner Organization (RPO) to help you conduct this gap analysis.

It's important to understand that a self-assessment is just to help you prepare. There is no "self-assessment score" when it comes to the actual certification. CMMC compliance requires a company to undergo an assessment by a certified CMMC Third Party Assessment Organization (C3PAO) to determine the level of security maturity achieved. The assessment is conducted based on the controls and practices outlined in the NIST SP 800-171 framework, as well as additional requirements specific to CMMC. The assessors will evaluate the implementation of each control and practice and assign a score for each level of security maturity. Therefore, achieving CMMC compliance requires an actual assessment by a certified third-party organization and cannot be determined through a self-assessment score.

8. **CMMC compliance can be a competitive advantage.** Without CMMC compliance, you will lose government contracts, which could put you out of business. But with CMMC, you not only are able to win government contracts but also provide reassurance to customers about your commitment to cybersecurity best practices, giving you a competitive advantage over vendors who aren't CMMC compliant.

CMMC isn't just to protect government secrets. Ultimately, if you are working with the DoD or are a vendor to them, you are an extremely active, valuable target.

My company partners with a firm in which the founder formerly worked for the National Security Agency (NSA). His job was to infiltrate foreign government computers and watch what they were doing without them knowing about it. When he realized that US companies were being compromised by foreign governments, he left the NSA and started a company to protect those companies. When we first partnered with the company, we deployed the product on 500 or so computers at thirty-five client firms that we were managing at the time. Three computers that we had no clue were compromised came back as infected. Can you guess what kind of company had the infected computers? All three were with DoD contractors. While individually, the pieces of information collected from a company might not mean much, when you put information together—grabbing a piece here and a piece there—it can be devastating. It's like putting a puzzle together, where eventually you have the whole picture. This demonstrates just how critical compliance is.

While achieving CMMC compliance is a significant undertaking, such compliance is crucial for companies working with the DoD. By understanding the requirements and working with a qualified MSP or MSSP, you can ensure your company is well-prepared and competitive when bidding on DoD contracts and protect your company and the US simultaneously.

About Craig

Craig Rabe is the founder and president of First Class Networks, known throughout Greater Boston for their highly responsive IT support, comprehensive cybersecurity strategies, and compliance assessments and implementations.

As an accomplished leader in IT services for over twenty-five years, Craig makes serving and protecting small and medium-sized businesses (SMBs) his top priority. Providing specialized IT and cybersecurity services, Craig and his team have helped SMBs maintain peak operation; stay protected against ransomware, hacks, attacks, data theft, and other vulnerabilities; and meet compliance regulations.

At age ten, Craig became fascinated with computers when his father, a civil engineer for the Air Force, brought home a TRS-80 computer. Craig spent hours on it, not just playing video games but also learning how to program and save programs onto audiotapes.

Upon receiving his degree in electrical and computer engineering from Clarkson University, he joined Arrow Electronics, selling semiconductors and computer systems to manufacturers.

After working for Arrow Electronics for four years, Craig was determined to fulfill a goal he had set when he was just eleven years old to own a business by his twenty-fifth birthday. Searching for the right opportunity, he discovered that computer novices were underserved. In 1996, using computers he'd assembled with Intel samples of the latest-generation computer processors, he opened the Computer Café when he was twenty-six years old. His new business provided computers to use with high-speed Internet, as well as hands-on computer training, computer sales, and repairs.

In 2013, after business owners repeatedly came to him for help managing their computers, Craig founded First Class Networks to provide local businesses with specialized managed IT services.

In 2018, Craig was inspired to up his cybersecurity game after reading an article in the *Washington Post* about how hackers had compromised the computers of a Navy contractor and stolen massive amounts of highly sensitive information. He recognized a correlation to increasing incidents of computer security breaches reported by local business owners who'd suffered thefts in the multimillions of dollars. Pooling all his resources, Craig doubled down on security, focusing his team's efforts on protecting the Boston-area SMB community against cybercrime while simultaneously continuing to provide superior IT support.

Craig subsequently built First Class Networks into a managed security services provider (MSSP), expanded his cybersecurity team, and is regarded as one of the foremost trusted experts in cybersecurity solutions and protection in Greater Boston. His team also evaluates network environments, provides complete assessments of overall security, and implements comprehensive security plans to meet compliance requirements that adhere to HIPAA, SOC, CMMC, and other regulations.

As a servant leader to his community, Craig has been honored as Entrepreneur of the Year in Arlington, Massachusetts. He's served twelve years on the board of the Winchester Chamber of Commerce and four years as the Chamber's president. Additionally, he served on the board of directors for the Boston chapter of the Entrepreneurs' Organization and as a member of the Winchester Rotary. Craig also helps families in need as a volunteer for Food Link, which has distributed over one million meals in the Boston area.

For more information, contact Craig at First Class Networks:

Email: craig@firstclassnetworks.com
Phone: (617) 209-3727 (Direct)
Web: www.firstclassnetworks.com
LinkedIn: www.linkedin.com/in/crabe

Chapter 25

WHY THE ANSWERS TO THESE SIXTEEN QUESTIONS CAN HELP YOU SELECT THE RIGHT IT PROVIDER

William Prusow

A t this point, digital processes and operations should be etched into the DNA of every business. So you would think we've moved beyond asking the question, "Why do I need an IT services provider?" In case you happen to be falling behind, here's a quick reminder. Running a successful business requires a complex and dynamic group of systems, networks, and applications to keep you efficient, competitive, and safe from cyberthreats. An IT services provider gives you a whole team of experts, including a help desk, technicians, and network engineers so you can focus on your primary business.[85] Now that you know you need a managed IT services provider, how do you find the RIGHT one?

Choosing an IT and computer support company isn't easy. There is no shortage of alarming stories about inexperienced IT "professionals" making critical mistakes and causing even bigger problems because of their incompetence.[86]

The IT consulting industry is—unfortunately—full of inept or unethical providers who take advantage of trusting business owners who don't have the ability to determine whether the technician knows what they're doing. And the provider certainly isn't going to offer up that they don't know what they're doing. When we take on new clients, there is always a story behind their previous computer service providers who were unreliable and difficult to reach and who "nickeled-and-dimed" them while failing to keep their network running properly and provide the level of service expected and needed.

Why are there so many unreliable, incapable IT services providers out there? Here's a little-known fact about the IT services industry: It is not regulated like many other professional service industries, which means ANYONE can claim they are an "IT expert." In fact, some computer technicians start their own businesses after being unsuccessful in an IT job and unable to find work elsewhere. Often, they are unqualified to provide comprehensive IT support services and lack the resources for the training required to become competent.

Automotive repair shops, electricians, plumbers, lawyers, Realtors, dentists, doctors, accountants, etc. are examples of professions that are regulated to protect consumers from receiving substandard work. But not the IT industry. It remains unregulated, without any laws in place to protect the consumer.

Anyone can promote themselves as a computer expert. Even if they are honestly trying to do a good job for you, an inexperienced or incompetent IT provider could result in devastating costs to your business, from lost productivity or even catastrophic data loss. The information in this chapter is intended to help raise standards within the IT support industry and give you useful information to help you avoid substandard IT services providers.

Who NOT to Hire

Most people look for a part-time "guru" for one reason: to save a few bucks. But this often comes back to haunt them. We frequently get calls from business owners who desperately need our help to get them back up and running or to clean up a mess that was caused by their nephew, neighbor's kid, brother-in-law, or friend who was just trying to help.

If the person you have working on your machine does not do IT support for a living, there is a good chance they won't have the knowledge or experience to truly help you—they are a hobbyist at best. And do you really want a part-time, inexperienced person responsible for handling something as important as your data and computer network? As with everything in life, you get what you pay for. That's not to say you need to go broke to find a great technician, but you shouldn't be choosing someone based on price alone.

Don't go into the search for a service provider thinking that all IT technicians are created equal and that your best option will be the one who offers the lowest price. **You get what you pay for.**

A cheap price usually means a cheap job. Really good technicians do NOT work cheaply because they are in high demand, just like every other professional service category. The only technicians who will work for a bargain price are those just starting out, and they are grossly inexperienced.

Some shops will hire college kids or newbie technicians because they will work for next to nothing to gain experience, OR they allow interns to support your network because they don't have to pay them at all—but what you don't realize is that an inexperienced technician like this can end up costing more because:

1. They improperly diagnose problems, which means you're paying them to fix the WRONG thing, and they STILL won't resolve your problem.
2. They could take three to five times as long to do the same repair an experienced technician could fix quickly. Again, you're paying for those extra hours.
3. They could do MORE damage, costing you more money and downtime. With your client data, accounting records, email, and other critical data at stake, do you REALLY want the lowest-priced shop working on your machine?

When it comes to selecting an IT services provider to support your business, it's important to compare their services directly. To help you in your search, I've put together these sixteen questions to ask a potential provider—and the answers you want to hear from them.

---

1. Do they answer their phones live, or do you have to leave a voicemail and wait for someone to call you back?
Answer: They should answer their calls live during the business hours they promised you.

2. Do they have a written, guaranteed response time to your calls?
Answer: Most IT services providers should be able to respond to you within thirty minutes or less after receiving your call for service. And if they need to be on-site, it should be the same business day, within a few hours. Make sure that is spelled out in your agreement.

3. Do they carry errors and omissions insurance as well as workers' compensation to protect your business?

Answer: What if an IT technician causes a problem with your network and, as a result, you're down for days or lose critical data? Who is responsible if a technician is injured while at your office? Adequate insurance coverage for both errors and omissions AND workers' compensation is essential to protecting your business. ANY responsible IT consulting firm will gladly provide proof of coverage.

4. Do they insist on remotely monitoring your network 24/7/365 to keep critical security settings, virus definitions, and security *patches up-to-date and PREVENT problems from turning into downtime, viruses, lost data, and other issues?*

Answer: The answer should be YES. Network monitoring systems watch over your network to constantly look for developing problems, security issues, and other problems so they can be addressed BEFORE they escalate.

5. Do they consistently (and proactively) offer new ways to improve your network's performance, or will they wait until you have a problem to make recommendations?

Answer: The IT provider should offer to schedule regular systems reviews with you to look for new ways to help improve your operations, increase efficiencies, lower costs, and resolve problems.

6. Do they guarantee to complete projects on time and on budget?

Answer: All projects should be fixed-priced and guaranteed to be completed on time, in writing. An unethical or incompetent IT provider will often quote "time and materials," which provides ample opportunity to "nickel-and-dime" you and linger longer than necessary because they are paid by the hour.

7. Do they INSIST on monitoring both an off-site and an on-site backup, or are they letting you rely on outdated tape backups or swapping out USB hard drives?

Answer: Tape backups should not be used because they are incredibly unreliable. USB sticks and portable USB hard drives are equally unreliable. Many companies forget to switch out the tapes or drives, and backups quickly become outdated and useless. Taking the backups off-site can compromise the security of your company data. The IT provider should make sure every client has both an on-site automated backup and a secure off-site backup.

8. Do they perform periodic test restores of your backups to make sure the data is not corrupt and can be restored in the event of a disaster?

Answer: They need to perform test restores from backups to make sure their data CAN be recovered in the event of an emergency. The worst time to "test" a backup is when you need to use it. They should, upon request, be able to provide you with a screenshot of a restored server or a report at least monthly to show that it is being done.

9. Do they insist on backing up your network BEFORE performing any type of project or upgrade?

Answer: Before beginning work on any server, workstation, or network device, they should make sure there is a good backup to rely on as a precaution in case a hardware failure or software glitch causes a major problem.

10. If you were to experience a major disaster, do they have a plan for how your data could be restored FAST and/or one that enables you to work from a remote location?

Answer: They should develop a disaster recovery plan for both your data and your networks.

11. Do they have their own help desk or, at the very least, a help desk based in the US?

Answer: In most cases, you get better support from a help desk that is owned by the IT provider, as their team will be familiar with how the IT provider operates. If the IT provider outsources their help desk to a third party, at the very least it should be US-based.

12. Do their technicians participate in ongoing training?

Answer: You don't want techs who are learning on YOUR job at YOUR business. They should be continually learning new products and keeping up with technology before they get to your business.

13. Does the IT provider offer you advanced security products such as EDR (endpoint detection and response), logging capabilities, next-generation antivirus, and a 24/7/365 security operation center option to monitor your environment and react in the event of an emergency? Additionally, ask if they are using the same advanced security products internally.

Answer: An IT provider must be able to offer you advanced security products and support them in order to protect you from threats. Also, they need to be using them internally as well, not only to protect themselves but also to protect you as their client. This way, you know they are knowledgeable about how the products work and that they trust them.

14. How many employees does the IT provider have, and is the number of staff adequate to service your business?

Answer: They need to have the proper levels of staff to address all your needs, including help desk support, on-site physical repair, field techs, and network engineers to troubleshoot and solve server issues.

15. Do they provide a system audit before they provide a quote?

Answer: They should. Invite them to your office. A competent professional should offer an audit of your network to diagnose your system BEFORE they give you a quote. Would you take a doctor's word that you need surgery if he had not done any diagnostics? Of course not! Prescription without diagnosis is malpractice.

16. Are they willing to give you references?

Answer: Don't choose an IT provider without speaking to several of their current clients.[87] Ask for three or four clients who have a business similar in size and scope to yours and check their references. Another good sign is that they should have multiple client testimonials and success stories posted on their website. A lack of this may be a sign that they don't HAVE clients who are happy enough to provide a good reference. If they hesitate or cannot provide you with references, move on.

Conclusion

A third-party IT services provider gives you access to the resources, experience, and knowledge that would take your internal team years to develop. Knowing whether a potential provider has what it takes to address your IT needs starts with asking the right questions—and getting the right answers.

About Bill

William "Bill" Prusow is the CEO and owner of Pros 4 Technology. The firm, located in Sheboygan Falls, Wisconsin, was founded in 2009 based on a desire to empower small businesses to drive economic success through technology.

Pros 4 Technology specializes in managed IT services, network security, computer and server repairs and upgrades, and network design for city and county governments, as well as small and medium-sized businesses, across several industries in Plymouth and Sheboygan.

Bill's expertise in IT began in 1989 when he started his first IT entrepreneurial endeavor. He specialized in computer consulting, computer sales and service, networking, and satellite headend systems for hospitals. He was one of the first Wisconsin-based companies to design and implement wireless data solutions, shepherding customers through technology changes from the earliest Internet connections to modern Wi-Fi systems. As an entrepreneur himself, Bill understands how small businesses run and what kind of IT support owners need to keep their systems operating optimally and within budget. Many of his clients have been with him for thirty years or more.

Today, Bill has grown Pros 4 Technology into one of Wisconsin's most trusted and reliable IT providers, serving clients with five to eight-hundred-plus workstations. His technical team of eighteen ranges from help desk support to network engineers—all carefully selected for their extensive knowledge of business technology systems and security—exceptional diagnostic skills, integrity and work ethic, and commitment to client satisfaction.

Bill holds a Bachelor of Business Administration from the University of Wisconsin-Milwaukee and has more than thirty-five years of experience in IT services.

He is the author of *What Every Business Owner Must Know About Hiring an Honest, Competent, Responsive, and Fairly Priced Computer Consultant*, the ultimate guide to finding the right IT provider partner.

Bill frequently shares his knowledge and expertise in the IT space, specifically by giving free cybersecurity speeches throughout the year for different organizations. When he's away from the office, he enjoys driving his Shelby Mustang and Harley-Davidson motorcycle, as well as fishing of all types.

For more information, contact Bill at Pros 4 Technology:

Email: bill.prusow@pros4tech.com

Phone: (920) 400-1279

Web: www.pros4technology.com

LinkedIn: www.linkedin.com/in/bill-prusow-3a44b11b

Address: 818 East Clifford Street, Plymouth, WI 53073

Chapter 26

HOW AN IT SERVICES PROVIDER KEEPS HER OWN KIDS SAFE ONLINE

Kari Renn

O dds are you're doing what you can to keep your business cyber-safe. But what are you doing outside of the office to protect your children from bad actors and cyberthreats while they're online? If you're being honest with yourself, now is the time to set aside those *Little House on the Prairie* false notions of comfort and get acquainted with the realities of today's digital environment.

Though Internet usage opens up a world of academic, social, and entertainment opportunities for kids, the dangerous side of online access can no longer be ignored. One minute your kids are researching something for school and the next they're falling down a rabbit hole of misinformation or chatting with strangers on a social media platform or online game. Know this: Every time your child is online, data is being collected, predators are prowling, cyberbullies are attacking, and bad actors are phishing. Scary thought, huh?

We can argue whose responsibility it is for making the Internet safer for kids—the government, tech companies, schools—but the truth is that everybody needs to ante up. And while we hold our collective breath for the "grown-ups" on Capitol Hill, the C-suite execs in Silicon Valley, or the greedy app developers across the globe to work together to create impactful legislation that makes the Internet safe for our children, teaching kids about online safety and security issues starts with parents NOW.

As the owner of a managed IT services provider firm, I make a living dealing with security management issues, and I've seen the resulting carnage when small and medium-sized businesses let their cyberguard down. And as a mother of teenagers who live and breathe by their technology, I find it nerve-racking that I can't know everything they're doing. The challenge lies in striking a balance between their privacy and being a good parent while teaching them to be responsible and safe digital citizens. For those of you facing the same struggle, I offer these seven pieces of advice I've put into practice with my own children.

1. Discuss Internet Safety Early . . . And Often

If you really want to fail as a parent, take the attitude that your children know all about the dangers lurking on the Internet and that they would never fall for a scam or predator. The fact is that people under the age of twenty have experienced the biggest year-over-year increase in online fraud.[88]

As soon as your children are old enough to interact with you while you're online and before they do anything online by themselves, begin the dialogue about Internet safety, online etiquette, and how to spot red flags of online predators (which we'll discuss later in this chapter).

When your kids turn into teenagers, there's a whole other set of headaches to worry about, like sexting and cyberbullying. Internet safety should never be a one-time conversation with your kids. Keep in mind that how they interact online and what apps and platforms they use are constantly changing, which brings me to the second piece of advice.

2. Teach Yourself About New Technology

As much as it might hurt to admit it, our kids are often more tech-savvy than we are. Trying to keep up with all the new apps, channels, and platforms they live on can be intimidating for a parent, but it's important to understand where they're going online and how they're using digital tools. Considering kids under the age of eight spend an average of two hours and nineteen minutes per day using mobile devices and teens spend over seven hours per day, you definitely better know what they're doing.[89]

Take the first step and learn what apps they're using, and then do some research to help you decide which ones are appropriate and safe for your children. There are TONS of parental control tools on the market that help you manage everything your child can access on their phone, computers, and gaming devices—essentially, anything connected to the Internet. You can block kids from browsing specific websites, downloading certain apps, and accessing social media, and you can even track and manage their screen time.

Of course, if you're parents of teens, you'll likely get the "you're-spying-on-me" argument or "I-can't-believe-you-don't-trust-me" squabble over control apps. This is what I remind my own kids: It's not about trusting you—because I do; it's about not trusting the people who can interact with you.

3. Warn Kids About Stranger Danger Online

You've warned your kids over and over in the real world—don't talk to strangers, don't accept gifts from strangers, don't get into a car with a stranger, and scream if a stranger tries to grab you. Unfortunately, predators also exist online, waiting to interact with children—over the Internet and in person.

Here's a sobering fact. There are an estimated 500,000 online predators who are active. Every. Single. Day.[90] They hide anonymously behind their screens, hanging out on social media, games, and chat rooms that are created for children and teens, looking for opportunities to groom and manipulate susceptible kids. Your kids assume they're talking to peers while these online predators gain their trust and slowly build a friendship. Here are a few red flags you and your children should be on the lookout for that could indicate their "friend" is actually a predator.

- They ask for a lot of personal information.
- They use adult phrases and make sexual jokes or statements.
- They promise favors and gifts if the child performs a certain task.
- They contact the child through multiple platforms and services.
- They want to talk privately offline.
- They have sparse online profiles with few posts and few "follows" or "friends."
- They tell the child to keep the relationship secret.
- They ask for photos and initiate intimate discussions about the child's appearance.
- They insist on meeting face-to-face.

It's also important to know that online predators may be someone you or your child knows in real life who is using the online world to become closer friends.

Parents, I feel your pain when it comes to having open and honest conversations with your children about sex and dating and body boundaries, but when you can maintain an open dialogue with your children about the associated risks of being online and the red flags, they're more likely to come to you if they think someone's behavior is questionable or makes them uncomfortable.

4. Write It, Post It, and It's Permanent

We all have digital footprints, those invisible "cookie crumbs" we leave behind every time we're online. The websites we browse, the photos and comments we post, the emails we send, the chats we create—all of these are snapshots of our online lives. The sad thing is this trail of data is here to stay. And that's not good news for our kids.

Considering the brain doesn't fully develop and mature until we're in our mid to late twenties, our kids will do some really, REALLY dumb things online in their teen years. You've probably seen news reports where a student posts a derogatory video about a teacher or another student on their social media platform and shares it with a "small group of close friends." Before you know it, the video becomes viral, and that student ends up losing a college scholarship over the incident.

Teens by nature are impulsive; that's why it's so important to remind them that their digital footprint can't be deleted. A lapse in judgment now can come back to bite them in the butt as adults when they're applying for college, looking for a job, or starting a relationship. As a parent, you can help ensure your child has a clean digital footprint by discouraging them from gossiping, bullying, or damaging someone else's reputation online. Also, talk to them about what is and isn't appropriate to share, such as compromising photographs or videos. Content and photos that are posted online can be altered or mispresented. And here's an important takeaway: Content that you share with a private group WILL more than likely be seen by people outside of that group. Here are some tips to help your kids protect their digital footprint.

- Change the privacy settings on social media to control who sees their posts.
- Avoid oversharing on social media.
- Delete unflattering content from your social media pages.
- Set cookie preferences and block third-party cookies.
- Share positive and uplifting stories and achievements.
- Think before you post!

5. Guard Personal Information Fiercely

Your children's personal information is valuable. That's why they need to limit the information they share on social media, online games, chat forums, and websites. They should never reveal their address, phone number, the school they go to, their birthday, or their location to anyone outside of their household. If they're using gaming devices, they should only use their screen name—never their real name. And they absolutely should not share passwords with anyone other than a parent.

The more information your children share online, the more vulnerable they become. A 2022 study found that one in forty-three American kids had their identities exposed in a data breach over the previous year.[91] Teens are attractive targets for identity thieves because they usually have a clean credit report or no credit at all, which means they aren't checking credit reports or scores. For that reason, I suggest checking your child's credit report when they're around the age of sixteen so that if their identity was stolen, you have time to fix it before they need it.

It's not just identity thieves you have to worry about. Online predators use the personal information your children share to stalk or exploit them. Teach your children to let you know immediately if someone asks for this personal information.

Because we live in the real world, we know kids aren't going to get our approval before sharing *everything* online, so just be upfront with them about your expectations of what they should and shouldn't share online. If you really want to scare them, remind them of tip #4.

6. Teach Your Kids Online Etiquette

You'll find exceptionally long lists of acceptable "netiquette" out there in cyberspace, but I have three golden rules I insist my children adhere to when they're online:

1. **Post only about others as you would expect them to post about you.** How children behave online can have a positive or a negative impact on other people. Inspire your children to be the ones who contribute to positivity and self-confidence in others.
2. **If you wouldn't say it in person, don't say it online.** It's easy for a kid to sit behind a screen and hammer out some mean, offensive, sarcastic, or controversial posts just so they can seem superior or interesting. Remind your child that if they have to hide to say it, then it shouldn't be said.

3. **Don't participate in heated online exchanges.** Debate is healthy, but if conversations get overly dramatic and tempers flare, then someone is going to say something they really don't mean, and once it's in writing, well . . . refer back to tip #4. Encourage your child to leave the online debate and vent offline to you or another family member until they've cooled down.

7. Allow Your Kids Some Freedom

Last but not least, we have to allow our kids the chance to become independent think-ers and doers while they're online. After all, we can't expect kids to get Internet safety right when adults fall victim to bad actors every day online! As I said at the beginning of this chapter, the challenge to keeping kids safe online lies in striking a balance between their privacy and being a good parent.

For my teens, I do have safeguards and parental controls in place. I can go in and see the history of the websites they're going to . . . if I want to. I may not check on them often, but it keeps them honest. They're less likely to go to sites or download apps that I wouldn't approve of because they know Mom could be watching. I think I'm doing them a better service as a parent if I help them understand the risks of being online and how to identify them than if I am telling them what to do.

Conclusion

As children spend more time online and begin doing so at an early age, communicat-ing with your child about online risks and how to stay safe is key. Sure, you're going to have to set some rules and perhaps put some parental controls in place, but when the lines of communication stay open, your children will feel more comfortable coming to you if they do have a bad or questionable online experience. And one final take-away—practice what you preach when it comes to your own online behavior.

About Kari

Kari Renn is the president and CEO of LoyalITy. The Green Bay, Wisconsin-based IT services firm was established in 2004 to help companies leverage technology to reach their business goals. LoyalITy is recognized as one of the top managed IT services providers in Wisconsin and Milwaukee, supporting numerous clients throughout the Midwest.

LoyalITy provides quality IT support for small to medium-sized businesses in the Green Bay and Fox Cities surrounding areas. The company's mission is to make information technology work at work so its clients can focus on their company goals without interruption.

Kari's interest in IT began after a successful career at Fox Converting as director of human resources. She eventually took over the company's IT department as vice president of operations. During her thirteen-year tenure with Fox Converting, Kari completed her Executive Master of Business Administration.

In 2018, after completing her EMBA, the opportunity to purchase and lead LoyalITy presented itself. Over the past five years, Kari's passion for innovation and success has helped drive LoyalITy forward. The business distinguishes itself from other regional MSPs by specializing in providing IT solutions tailored to the needs of business-oriented individuals seeking growth, enhanced productivity, and tools to facilitate their business advancement.

Kari earned a Bachelor of Arts from the University of Wisconsin-Green Bay and her executive MBA from the University of Wisconsin-Oshkosh.

Outside the office, Kari can be found reading, especially books about business or mystery and action-adventure novels, when she truly wants to unwind. She is also a history buff and enjoys traveling with her family.

For more information, contact Kari at LoyalITy:

Email: krenn@loyality.com
Phone: (920) 489-3187
Web: www.loyality.com
LinkedIn: www.linkedin.com/in/kari-renn-b471b058/
Address: 200 Packerland Dr., Green Bay, WI 54303

ENDNOTES

1 "Modern Bank Heist 5.0, The Escalation: From Heist to Hijack, From Dwell to Destruction," VMware, August 24, 2023, https://www.vmware.com/learn/security/1414485_REG.html.

2 "43% of Cyberattacks Target Small Businesses," *CISION PRNewswire*, October 11, 2018, https://prnewswire.com/news-releases/43-of-cyberattacks-target-small-businesses-300729384.html.

3 Andrew Rinaldi, "The Cost of Cybersecurity and How to Budget for It," Business.com, August 2023, https://www.business.com/articles/smb-budget-for-cybersecurity.

4 "Spear Phishing: Top Threats and Trends," Barracuda Networks, March 2019, https://www.barracuda.com/reports/spear-phishing-report.

5 "BullGuard: New Study Reveals One in Three SMBs Use Free Consumer Cybersecurity and One in Five Use No Endpoint Security at All," *CISION: PRNewswire*, February 19, 2020, https://www.prnewswire.com/news-releases/bullguard-new-study-reveals-one-in-three-smbs-use-free-consumer-cybersecurity-and-one-in-five-use-no-endpoint-security-at-all-301007466.html.

6 "BullGuard: New Study Reveals," *CISION: PRNewswire*.

7 Kevin Ocasio, "43 Small Business Cybersecurity Statistics," *Small Business Trends*, May 29, 2023, https://smallbiztrends.com/2023/05/small-business-cybersecurity.html.

8 "2023 MSP Benchmark Survey Report: MSP Industry Trends," Kaseya, April 12, 2023, https://www.kaseya.com/resource/2023-msp-benchmark-survey-report/.

9   Jeremy Spivey, "Hackers Wait Up to Six Months After Access to Trigger Ransomware," WingSwept, July 29, 2020, https://www.wingswept.com/hackers-wait-months-after-network-access-to-trigger-ransomware/.

10 Spivey, "Hackers Wait to Trigger Ransomware."

11 "History of Computer Viruses: Creeper and Reaper.," *Pandora FMS Monitoring Blog*, April 25, 2023, https://pandorafms.com/blog/creeper-and-reaper/.

12 "The History of Cyber Security—Everything You Ever Wanted to Know," *SentinelOne Blog*, February 10, 2019, https://www.sentinelone.com/blog/history-of-cyber-security.

13 Steve Morgan, "Cybercrime To Cost The World $10.5 Trillion Annually By 2025," *Cybercrime Magazine*, November 13, 2020, https://cybersecurityventures.com/hackerpocalypse-cybercrime-report-2016.

14 *Internet Crime Report 2020*, Federal Bureau of Investigation, https://www.ic3.gov/Media/PDF/AnnualReport/2020_IC3Report.pdf.

15 *2022 Data Breach Investigations Report*, Verizon, May 24, 2022, https://www.verizon.com/business/resources/T5a6/reports/dbir/2022-data-breach-investigations-report-dbir.pdf.

16 Melissa Angell, "Most Businesses Don't Survive Ransomware Attacks. What to Do in the Aftermath to Soften the Blow," Inc.com, April 25, 2020, https://www.inc.com/melissa-angell/ransomware-attack-small-medium-sized-business-prepare.html.

17 Steve Morgan, "Cyberwarfare in the C-Suite," *Cybercrime Magazine*, November 13, 2020, https://cybersecurityventures.com/hackerpocalypse-cybercrime-report-2016/.

18 Robert Johnson III, "60 Percent of Small Companies Close Within 6 Months of Being Hacked," *Cybercrime Magazine*, January 2, 2019, https://cybersecurityventures.com/60-percent-of-small-companies-close-within-6-months-of-being-hacked/.

19 Sally Adam, "The State of Ransomware 2022," Sophos News, April 27, 2022, https://news.sophos.com/en-us/2022/04/27/the-state-of-ransomware-2022/.

20 "IBM Report: Cost of a Data Breach Hits Record High during Pandemic," IBM Newsroom, July 28, 2021, https://newsroom.ibm.com/2021-07-28-IBM-Report-Cost-of-a-Data-Breach-Hits-Record-High-During-Pandemic.

21 Branko Krstic, "15+ Scary Data Loss Statistics to Keep in Mind in 2023," Web-Tribunal, May 20, 2023, https://webtribunal.net/blog/data-loss-statistics.

22 "Cybereason Ransomware True Cost to Business Study Reveals Organizations Pay Multiple Ransom Demands," Cybereason.com, June 7, 2022, https://www.cybereason.com/press/cybereason-ransomware-true-cost-to-business-study-reveals-organizations-pay-multiple-ransom-demands.

23 "Major US CFPB Data Breach Caused by Employee," Dark Reading, April 20, 2023, https://www.darkreading.com/attacks-breaches/major-us-cfpb-data-breach-employee.

24 Anna Zhadan, "World Economic Forum Finds That 95% of Cybersecurity Incidents Occur Due to Human Error," CyberNews, January 18, 2022, https://cybernews.com/editorial/world-economic-forum-finds-that-95-of-cybersecurity-incidents-occur-due-to-human-error/.

25 David Tidmarsh, "What Is Spear Phishing and How Can You Prevent It," EC-Council Cybersecurity Exchange, April 12, 2023, https://www.eccouncil.org/cybersecurity-exchange/ethical-hacking/what-is-spear-phishing-examples-types-prevention.

26 Jenny Chang, "55 Important Password Statistics You Should Know: 2023 Breaches & Reuse Data," Financesonline.com, last modified September 2023, https://financesonline.com/password-statistics.

27 Jenny Chang, "55 Important Password Statistics You Should Know: 2023 Breaches & Reuse Data," Financesonline.com, last modified September 2023, https://financesonline.com/password-statistics.

28 "A Brief History of Cybercrime," Arctic Wolf, November 16, 2022, https://arcticwolf.com/resources/blog/decade-of-cybercrime.

29 *Jimmy Kimmel Live*, "What Is Your Password?," January 16, 2015, https://www.youtube.com/watch?v=opRMrEfAIiI.

30 Oracle Mind, "This Is How Hackers Hack You Using Simple Social Engineering," May 1, 2016, https://www.youtube.com/watch?v=lc7scxvKQOo.

31 *2022 Data Breach Investigations Report*, Verizon, May 24, 2022, https://www.verizon.com/business/resources/T369/reports/dbir/2022-data-breach-investigations-report-dbir.pdf.

32 Shweta Sharma, "Microsoft Takes Top Spot as Most Impersonated Brand in Phishing," *CSO Online*, July 28, 2022, https://www.csoonline.com/

article/573323/microsoft-takes-top-spot-as-most-impersonated-brand-in-phishing.html.

33 Stu Sjouwerman, "Train Employees and Cut Cyber Risks Up To 70 Percent," *KnowBe4 Blog*, https://blog.knowbe4.com/train-employees-and-cut-cyber-risks-up-to-70-percent.

34 Paul Mee and Rico Brandenburg, "After Reading, Writing and Arithmetic, the 4th 'R' of Literacy Is Cyber-Risk," World Economic Forum, December 17, 2020, https://www.weforum.org/agenda/2020/12/cyber-risk-cyber-security-education.

35 "The Biggest Cyber Security Threats 2022," Coro, https://go.coro.net/cyber-threats2022.

36 Kif Leswing, "A Password for the Hawaii Emergency Agency Was Hiding in a Public Photo, Written on a Post-It Note," *Business Insider*, January 16, 2018, https://www.businessinsider.com/hawaii-emergency-agency-password-discovered-in-photo-sparks-security-criticism-2018-1.

37 Maria Korolov, "27% of US Office Workers Would Sell Their Passwords," CSO Online, March 21, 2016, https://www.csoonline.com/article/3046117/27-of-us-office-workers-would-sell-their-passwords.html.

38 "How to Create a Security Awareness Program That Employees Will Enjoy," CyberTalk, September 29, 2021, https://www.cybertalk.org/2021/09/29/how-to-create-a-security-awareness-program-that-employees-will-enjoy.

39 Sam Scholefield and Lynsay Shepherd, "Gamification Techniques for Raising Cyber Security Awareness," ResearchGate, March 20, 2019, https://www.researchgate.net/publication/331916014_Gamification_Techniques_for_Raising_Cyber_Security_Awareness.

40 Leslie Lau, "How Cisco Drives Social Media Training with Gamification," Gamification.co, February 5, 2014, https://www.gamification.co/2014/02/05/cisco-drives-social-media-training-gamification.

41 Jeanne C. Meister, "How Deloitte Made Learning a Game," Harvard Business Review, January 2, 2013, https://hbr.org/2013/01/how-deloitte-made-learning-a-g.

42 *Serious Gaming: The Security Awareness Escape* Room (Deloitte Risk Advisory, 2020), https://www2.deloitte.com/content/dam/Deloitte/nl/Documents/risk/deloitte-nl-cyber-risk-the-security-awareness-escape-room.pdf.

43 "Level Up Your Security Awareness with Cyber Games," Terranova Security, September 8, 2023, https://terranovasecurity.com/security-awareness-cyber-games/.

44 Tyler Schultz, "Gamification—Cybersecurity's Turn to Play," Infosec, January 18, 2021, https://resources.infosecinstitute.com/topics/industry-insights/gamification-cybersecurity-training.

45 Tommy Van Steen and Julia R.A. Deeleman, "Successful Gamification of Cybersecurity Training," *Cyberpsychology, Behavior, and Social Networking* 24, no. 9 (September 1, 2021): 593–98, https://doi.org/10.1089/cyber.2020.0526.

46 "5 Reasons Why You Need Gamification In Your Cyber Security Awareness Program," Terranova Security, August 4, 2023, https://terranovasecurity.com/reasons-you-need-gamification-in-security-awareness/.

47 "Does Gamification Inspire Intrinsic Motivation?," *Growth Engineering Blog*, March 6, 2019, https://www.growthengineering.co.uk/intrinsic-motivation-gamification.

48 Shane Snow, "Science Shows: Humans Have Massive Capacity for Sustained Attention, and Storytelling Unlocks It," *Forbes*, January 16, 2023, https://www.forbes.com/sites/shanesnow/2023/01/16/science-shows-humans-have-massive-capacity-for-sustained-attention-and-storytelling-unlocks-it.

49 Corey Bleich, "5 Benefits of Experiential Learning in the Workplace," *EdgePoint Learning Blog*, 2023, https://www.edgepointlearning.com/blog/benefits-of-experiential-learning.

50 Aris Apostolopoulos, "The 2019 Gamification at Work Survey," *TalentLMS Blog*, August 19, 2019, https://www.talentlms.com/blog/gamification-survey-results/.

51 "The Psychology of Human Error 2020," Tessian, March 29, 2022, https://www.tessian.com/research/the-psychology-of-human-error.

52 Scott Ikeda, "Study Shows Ransomware Attacks Down 61% In 2022, but Average Costs Remain High," *CPO Magazine*, January 7, 2023, https://www.cpomagazine.com/cyber-security/study-shows-ransomware-attacks-down-61-in-2022-but-average-costs-remain-high.

53 "FBI Investigates Hack of Its Own Computer Network," *Reuters*, February 17, 2023, https://www.reuters.com/world/us/fbi-says-it-has-contained-cyber-incident-bureaus-computer-network-cnn-2023-02-17.

54 "Kaseya Appoints Former FBI Special Agent Jason Manar as Chief Information Security Officer," Kaseya, October 18, 2021, https://www.kaseya.com/press-release/kaseya-appoints-former-fbi-special-agent-jason-manar-as-chief-information-security-officer.

55 *Cost of a Data Breach Report 2022* (IBM Security, 2022), https://www.ibm.com/downloads/cas/3R8N1DZJ.

56 "What All Businesses Should Know about Cyber Hygiene," *Tulane University Blog*, 2021, https://sopa.tulane.edu/blog/cyber-hygiene.

57 Alessandro Mascellino, "Global Cyber Attacks Rise by 7% in Q1 2023," *Infosecurity Magazine*, April 28, 2023, https://www.infosecurity-magazine.com/news/global-cyber-attacks-rise-7-q1-2023.

58 Mascellino, "Global Cyber Attacks Rise by 7% in Q1 2023."

59 "U.S. Cyber Insurance Market Update (Sharp Pricing Increases Yield Strong Profit Improvement)," Fitch Ratings, May 12, 2023, https://www.fitchratings.com/research/insurance/us-cyber-insurance-market-update-sharp-pricing-increases-yield-strong-profit-improvement-12-05-2023.

60 *2022 Data Breach Investigations Report*, Verizon, May 24, 2022, https://www.verizon.com/business/en-gb/resources/2022-data-breach-investigations-report-dbir.pdf.

61 "PwC Pulse Survey: Managing Business Risks," PwC, 2022, https://www.pwc.com/us/en/library/pulse-survey/managing-business-risks.html.

62 *Cost of a Data Breach Report 2022* (IBM Security, 2022), https://www.ibm.com/downloads/cas/3R8N1DZJ.

63 Steve Morgan, "Cybercrime to Cost the World 8 Trillion Annually in 2023," *Cybercrime Magazine*, October 17, 2022, https://cybersecurityventures.com/cybercrime-to-cost-the-world-8-trillion-annually-in-2023.

64 "The True Cost of Compliance with Data Protection Regulations | Ponemon Institute," Globalscape, December 1, 2017, https://www.globalscape.com/resources/whitepapers/data-protection-regulations-study.

65 Stephanie Kelly and Jessica Resnick-Ault, "One Password Allowed Hackers to Disrupt Colonial Pipeline, CEO Tells Senators," *Reuters*, June 8, 2021, https://www.reuters.com/business/colonial-pipeline-ceo-tells-senate-cyber-defenses-were-compromised-ahead-hack-2021-06-08.

66 Jack Koziol and Rob Watts, "Top 5 Cybersecurity Questions For Small Businesses Answered," *Forbes Advisor*, June 13, 2022, https://www.forbes.com/advisor/business/software/cybersecurity-questions-for-small-businesses-answered.

67 Maddie Shepherd, "30 Surprising Small Business Cyber Security Statistics," *Fundera*, January 23, 2023, https://www.fundera.com/resources/small-business-cyber-security-statistics.

68 "Data Breach Response: A Guide for Business," Federal Trade Commission, February 2021, https://www.ftc.gov/business-guidance/resources/data-breach-response-guide-business.

69 Bill Chappell, "Uber Pays $148 Million Over Yearlong Cover-Up Of Data Breach," *NPR*, September 27, 2018, https://www.npr.org/2018/09/27/652119109/uber-pays-148-million-over-year-long-cover-up-of-data-breach.

70 "Majority of Consumers Would Stop Doing Business with Companies Following a Data Breach, Finds Gemalto," Thales Group, November 28, 2017, https://www.thalesgroup.com/en/markets/digital-identity-and-security/press-release/majority-of-consumers-would-stop-doing-business-with-companies-following-a-data-breach-finds-gemalto.

71 Prajeet Nair, "Colonial Pipeline May Have to Pay Fine of Nearly $1 Million," BankInfoSecurity, May 10, 2022, https://www.bankinfosecurity.com/colonial-pipeline-may-have-to-pay-nearly-1-million-fine-a-19050.

72 Amy Martinez, "Data-Breach Settlements and Cyber-Security Lawsuits | Cyber-Security," *Florida Trend*, January 25, 2019, https://www.floridatrend.com/print/article/26215.

73 Elizabeth Snell, "Class-Action Lawsuit Filed after Allscripts Ransomware Attack," *HealthITSecurity*, January 30, 2018, https://healthitsecurity.com/news/class-action-lawsuit-filed-after-allscripts-ransomware-attack.

74 Bull Guard, "New Study Reveals One in Three SMBs Use Free Consumer Cybersecurity and One in Five Use No Endpoint Security at All," *CISION PRWeb*, February 19, 2020, https://www.prweb.com/releases/new_study_reveals_one_in_three_smbs_use_free_consumer_cybersecurity_and_one_in_five_use_no_endpoint_security_at_all/prweb16921507.htm.

75 Laura Wronski, "CNBC|SurveyMonkey Small Business Index Q2 2022," SurveyMonkey, April 2022, https://www.surveymonkey.com/curiosity/cnbc-small-business-q2-2022.

76 "Big Game Hunting Is Back Despite Decreasing Ransom Payment Amounts," Coveware, April 30, 2023, https://www.coveware.com/blog/2023/4/28/big-game-hunting-is-back-despite-decreasing-ransom-payment-amounts.

77 Kevin Ocasio, "43 Small Business Cybersecurity Statistics," *Small Business Trends*, May 29, 2023, https://smallbiztrends.com/2023/05/small-business-cybersecurity.html.

78 *The Global Risks Report 2022, 17th Edition*, World Economic Forum, January 11, 2023, https://www3.weforum.org/docs/WEF_The_Global_Risks_Report_2022.pdf.

79 "US Cyber Insurance Payouts Increase Amid Rising Claims, Premium Hikes," Fitch Ratings, May 6, 2022, https://www.fitchratings.com/research/insurance/us-cyber-insurance-payouts-increase-amid-rising-claims-premium-hikes-06-05-2022.

80 Anna Zhadan, "World Economic Forum Finds That 95% of Cybersecurity Incidents Occur Due to Human Error," CyberNews, January 18, 2022, https://cybernews.com/editorial/world-economic-forum-finds-that-95-of-cybersecurity-incidents-occur-due-to-human-error.

81 Saheed Oladimeji and Sean Michael Kerner, "Solarwinds Hack Explained: Everything You Need to Know," TechTarget, June 27, 2023, https://www.techtarget.com/whatis/feature/SolarWinds-hack-explained-Everything-you-need-to-know.

82 Ashwin Rodrigues, "Ransomware Attacks Are Part of the Cost of Doing Business," *Morning Brew*, May 5, 2022, https://www.morningbrew.com/daily/stories/ransomware-attacks-cost-of-business.

83 Linda Comerford, "Why Small Businesses Are Vulnerable to Cyberattacks," *Security Magazine*, May 25, 2022, https://www.securitymagazine.com/blogs/14-security-blog/post/97694-why-small-businesses-are-vulnerable-to-cyberattacks.

84 Daniel Gonzales, et al., "Unclassified and Secure: A Defense Industrial Base Cyber Protection Program for Unclassified Defense Networks," RAND Corporation, March 30, 2020, https://www.rand.org/pubs/research_reports/RR4227.html.

85 "11 Signs A Company Should Outsource IT," *Forbes*, April 10, 2019, https://www.forbes.com/sites/forbestechcouncil/2019/04/10/11-signs-a-company-should-outsource-it.

86 Anonymous, "3 Terrible Tales from the Tech Cleanup Crew," InfoWorld, November 5, 2014, https://www.infoworld.com/article/2843336/3-terrible-tales-tech-cleanup-crew.html.

87 Adam Burns, "Vet a Provider Thoroughly Before Signing on with an MSP," *SC Media*, September 23, 2021, https://www.scmagazine.com/perspective/third-party-risk/vet-a-provider-thoroughly-before-signing-on-with-an-msp.

88 Sarah O'Brien, "Tech-Savvy Teens Falling Prey to Online Scams Faster than Their Grandparents," *CNBC*, August 10, 2021, https://www.cnbc.com/2021/08/10/tech-savvy-teens-falling-prey-to-online-scams-faster-than-their-grandparents.html.

89 "The Top Apps Parents Should Know Their Kids Are Using," CentraCom, May 18, 2022, https://centracom.com/news/post/192/the-top-apps-parents-should-know-their-kids-are-using.

90 Kathryn Kosmides, "Online Platforms Have a Responsibility to Protect Children from Harm," TechCrunch, October 31, 2021, https://techcrunch.com/2021/10/31/online-platforms-have-a-responsibility-to-protect-children-from-harm.

91 "1.7 Million U.S. Children Fell Victim to Data Breaches, According to Javelin's 2022 Child Identity Fraud Study," Javelin Strategy & Research, October 26, 2022, https://javelinstrategy.com/press-release/17-million-us-children-fell-victim-data-breaches-according-javelins-2022-child.

Printed in the USA
CPSIA information can be obtained
at www.ICGtesting.com
JSHW022300080424
60798JS00004B/121

9 781636 983851